CAMBRIDGE LIBRARY COLLECTION

Books of enduring scholarly value

Spiritualism and Esoteric Knowledge

Magic, superstition, the occult sciences and esoteric knowledge appear regularly in the history of ideas alongside more established academic disciplines such as philosophy, natural history and theology. Particularly fascinating are periods of rapid scientific advances such as the Renaissance or the nineteenth century which also see a burgeoning of interest in the paranormal among the educated elite. This series provides primary texts and secondary sources for social historians and cultural anthropologists working in these areas, and all who wish for a wider understanding of the diverse intellectual and spiritual movements that formed a backdrop to the academic and political achievements of their day. It ranges from works on Babylonian and Jewish magic in the ancient world, through studies of sixteenth-century topics such as Cornelius Agrippa and the rapid spread of Rosicrucianism, to nineteenth-century publications by Sir Walter Scott and Sir Arthur Conan Doyle. Subjects include astrology, mesmerism, spiritualism, theosophy, clairvoyance, and ghost-seeing, as described both by their adherents and by sceptics.

Science and a Future Life

Frederic William Henry Myers (1843–1901) was a classical scholar who in mid-career turned to the investigation of psychic phenomena. After studying, and later teaching, Classics at Trinity College, Cambridge he resigned his lectureship in 1869, became an inspector of schools, and campaigned for women's higher education. With the encouragement of former colleagues he began a scientific investigation of spiritualism and related phenomena, and in 1882 he helped to found the Society for Psychical Research. This volume, first published in 1893, is a collection of essays that Myers had previously published in journals. Their topics include Charles Darwin's religious beliefs, the capacity of contemporary scientific methods to investigate the existence of the soul after death, and an unusual interpretation of Alfred Tennyson's poetry. These fascinating essays show how Myers engaged with the scientific developments and intellectual currents of his time as he developed his theory of the 'subliminal self'.

Cambridge University Press has long been a pioneer in the reissuing of out-of-print titles from its own backlist, producing digital reprints of books that are still sought after by scholars and students but could not be reprinted economically using traditional technology. The Cambridge Library Collection extends this activity to a wider range of books which are still of importance to researchers and professionals, either for the source material they contain, or as landmarks in the history of their academic discipline.

Drawing from the world-renowned collections in the Cambridge University Library, and guided by the advice of experts in each subject area, Cambridge University Press is using state-of-the-art scanning machines in its own Printing House to capture the content of each book selected for inclusion. The files are processed to give a consistently clear, crisp image, and the books finished to the high quality standard for which the Press is recognised around the world. The latest print-on-demand technology ensures that the books will remain available indefinitely, and that orders for single or multiple copies can quickly be supplied.

The Cambridge Library Collection will bring back to life books of enduring scholarly value (including out-of-copyright works originally issued by other publishers) across a wide range of disciplines in the humanities and social sciences and in science and technology.

Science and a Future Life

With Other Essays

FREDERIC WILLIAM HENRY MYERS

CAMBRIDGE
UNIVERSITY PRESS

CAMBRIDGE UNIVERSITY PRESS

Cambridge, New York, Melbourne, Madrid, Cape Town, Singapore,
São Paolo, Delhi, Dubai, Tokyo, Mexico City

Published in the United States of America by Cambridge University Press, New York

www.cambridge.org
Information on this title: www.cambridge.org/9781108027380

© in this compilation Cambridge University Press 2011

This edition first published 1893
This digitally printed version 2011

ISBN 978-1-108-02738-0 Paperback

SCIENCE AND A FUTURE LIFE

SCIENCE

AND

A FUTURE LIFE

WITH OTHER ESSAYS

BY

FREDERIC W. H. MYERS

London

MACMILLAN AND CO.

AND NEW YORK

1893

CONTENTS

THE Essays here reprinted, with due acknowledg-
ment, from the *Nineteenth Century* and the *Fort-
nightly Review* were not composed as a consecutive
series. They have, however, a certain unity of purpose,
which I have emphasised by placing first the Essay in
which this purpose is most plainly expressed. The
Essay on "The Disenchantment of France" is now
five years old, but I have let it stand unaltered, leaving my readers to decide how far its diagnosis has
been justified by subsequent history.

SCIENCE AND A FUTURE LIFE

To the question, " What has science to say as to man's survival of death ? " the chief spokes-men of modern science are inclined to answer, " Nothing at all." The affirmative answer she holds as unproved, and the negative answer as unprovable.

Nevertheless, in spite of, and by reason of, her studied neutrality, the influence of science is every year telling more strongly against a belief in a future life. Inevitably so ; since whatever science does not tend to prove, she in some sort tends to disprove ; beliefs die out, without formal refutation, if they find no place among the copious store of verified and systematised facts and inferences which are supplanting the traditions and speculations of

B

pre-scientific days as the main mental pabulum
of mankind.

And the very magnitude of the special
belief in question renders it, in one sense, the
more easily starved. Men feel that, if it were
true, there would surely be far more to be said
for it than they have ever heard. The silence
which surrounds the topic is almost more dis-
couraging than overt attack. At first, indeed,
in the early days of the scientific dominion,
savants were wont to make some sort of
apology, or disclaimer of competence, when
their doctrines seemed too obviously to ignore
man's hope of a future. Then came open
assaults from audacious and confident *savants*
—to whom the apologetic and optimistic
savants seemed to have nothing particular to
reply. And gradually the educated world—
that part of it, at least, which science leads—
is waking up to find that no mere trifles or
traditions only, but the great hope which inspired their fathers aforetime, is insensibly
vanishing away.

Now it is important that a question so
momentous should not thus be suffered to go
by default. There should be an occasional

stocktaking of evidence, an occasional inquiry whether, among the multifarious advances of science, any evidence has been discovered bearing on a question which, after all, is to science a question of evidence alone.

It seems to me that, even during this generation—even during the last few years—discoveries have, in fact, been made which must gradually revolutionise our whole attitude towards the question of an unseen world, and of our own past, present, or future existence therein.

Some of the discoveries of which I speak—in the realm of automatism and of human personality — have already commanded wide scientific assent, although their drift and meaning have, as I hold, been as yet very imperfectly understood. Other discoveries, which I regard as equally valid, are as yet disputed or ignored ; but they are, in fact, so closely linked with what is already admitted, that all analogy (I think) leads us to suppose that, in some form or other, these newer views also are destined profoundly to modify scientific thought.

The discoveries of which I speak are not

the result of any startling novelties of method. Rather, they are examples of the fruitful results which will often follow from the simple application of well-known methods of research to a group of phenomena which, for some special historical reason, has hitherto been left outside the steady current of experiment and observation.

Now, the whole inquiry into man's survival has thus far, if I may so say, fallen between two stools. Neither those who support the thesis, nor those who impugn it, have thus far made any serious attempt to approach it by scientific method.

On the one hand, materialistic science has, naturally enough, preferred to treat the subject as hardly capable of argument. There is the obvious fact that, when a man dies, you hear nothing more from him. And there is the fact—less obvious, indeed, but more and more fully established—that to every mental change some cerebral change corresponds ; with the inference that, when the brain decays, the mind is extinct as well.

This strong negative argument forms the basis of the popular treatises—Büchner's *Kraft*

und Stoff and *Das künftige Leben* may serve as
examples—which urge mankind definitely to
set aside all thought of a life to come.   The
argument is, necessarily, a purely negative one ;
it rests on the absence of positive testimony to
any mental energy with which some cerebral
change is not directly concomitant.   The
negative presumption will, therefore, be *shaken*
if accepted notions as to man's personality are
shown to be gravely defective, while it will be
at once *overthrown* if positive evidence to man's
survival of bodily death can in any way be
acquired.

To the arguments of Materialism, Philosophy
and Religion have replied in ways of their
own.   As regards the nature of human personality, philosophy has had much to say ; and
man's immortality has been the very corner
stone of the Christian faith.   But, with rare
exceptions, neither philosophy nor religion has
discovered, or even sought for, facts and arguments which could meet materialistic science
on its own ground.   The spokesmen of religion,
indeed, have generally preferred, for ecclesiastical or for moral reasons, to leave the
question of man's survival, or, as they have

termed it, man's immortality, to the domain of
faith.   On ecclesiastical grounds, they have
naturally desired to retain the monopoly of
spiritual teaching ; they have been less concerned to prove by carnal methods that an
unseen world exists, than to impress their own
crowning message or revelation upon men who
already believed in that world as a reality.
On moral grounds, also, they have felt it
dangerous to allow a dogma so essential as
man's future life to be thrown into the chaldron
of speculation.   So long, indeed, as the earthly
prosperity of the righteous was held sufficient
to prove the moral government of the world,
man's destiny after death might remain an
open field for primitive questionings.   But
when earthly justice was too plainly seen to
fail, then the doctrine of future reward and
punishment became necessary in order to
justify the ways of God to men.

Since, then, the thesis of man's survival has
been far oftener defended with an ethical than
with a merely scientific interest, it is no wonder
that the moral and emotional arguments should
have assumed almost complete predominance.

With those arguments I have in this essay

nothing to do. I am expressly laying aside all
support which the belief in a future life receives
either from " natural religion," from philosophy,
or from revelation. I wish to debate the
matter on the ground of experiments and
observations such as are appealed to in other
inquiries for definite objective proof.

Yet there is one argument which, since it is
historical as well as religious, I must not avoid
altogether. It will be urged by many readers
that the Resurrection of Christ is " a fact as
well attested as any in history "—better attested,
they will say, than many of the recent observations on which I rely. And although on that
historical question my opinion has no special
value, I must not shirk this appeal. I will say,
then, that I still adhere to Paley's view ; that I
cannot explain that testimony given by the
" twelve men of probity," in face of bonds and
stripes and death, except on the supposition that
Christ did in fact in some way manifest Himself
to His disciples after bodily life was extinct.
But I personally could not press this argument
upon other minds. I recognise that, were I
not convinced also of those facts of modern
occurrence which are actually in dispute, then,

although I might have a *moral* right, I should hardly have a *scientific* right to pin my faith to an event so marvellous and so isolated, and dating back to a time and country with standards of historical accuracy so different from our own.

And I observe that, among the newer school of theologians, there is less and less disposition to press the argument on purely historical grounds. Preachers do not often say, " Apart from all question of what Christ was or did, we have absolute proof that He rose from the dead, and, consequently, that all men are so constituted that they will rise also." Rather they say, " Christ sealed a divine life with this great manifestation of divinity ; therefore, we must believe Him when He tells us that we shall rise again."

It is natural enough to mix historical with moral proof where the purely moral elements in the demonstration have so often been found convincing. Yet it would be a grave mistake to suppose that, however cogent the moral proof of any proposition as to matter of fact may be, a scientific proof is thereby rendered superfluous. A belief which a man cannot

connect and correlate with other beliefs relating
to similar matters cannot long maintain an independent vitality.

As I have already said, the habit of belief
on definite scientific grounds tends to the
atrophy of all beliefs on matters of fact which
cannot be verified by rigorous historical methods,
or by modern experiment and observation.
Physical science is in this way far more scep-
tical—or, rather, far more agnostic—than Law.
Law has to act on probabilities ; it gives
weight to moral considerations when definite
proof cannot be had. But science, if definite
proof is unattainable, puts the matter aside
altogether.

The result is, as we all know, that the great
majority of Continental *savants* and disciples of
science have practically ceased to regard a
future life as a possibility worth discussing.
In England and America the case is different ;
but even here the belief in survival seems now
to rest, not so much on any definite creed,
as on a temper of mind which in energetic
Western races survives for some time the decay
of definite dogma. I mean that view of the
universe loosely styled optimism, but which

some now term *bonism*, with no greater bar-
barism in the form of the word, and more
accuracy in its meaning.   These sanguine
races, I say, still maintain their trust that the
Cosmos, as a whole, is good, even when the
definite beliefs on which this trust anciently
rested have one by one been cut away.   "We
cannot believe," they say, "that God or Nature
will put us to permanent intellectual confusion."
"We must hold that life has a meaning, and
that man's highest instincts are in accordance
with the truth of things."

One must needs feel sympathy for the
various groups, semi-Christian, Theistic, or
Pantheistic, who are thus striving to support,
on less and less of substantive aliment, the
spiritual life within.   But, alas! no sooner have
the Positivist school succeeded in reducing that
aliment to a large H in Humanity—the
spiritual equivalent of a straw *per diem*—than
the optimistic temper is found to be starved
out, and the Western world to be gravitating
towards the immemorial melancholy of the
East.

It is the pessimists who contribute the most
characteristic note to the philosophy of our

generation. They tell us that the young vigour of Western races has thus far accepted without question the illusive brightness which Nature's witchery casts upon human fates. But, as these races attain maturity of meditation, they will pass from under the magic spell; their restless energy will die down as it recognises that all energies in the end are vain.

Yet it is not in philosophical utterance, but in practical life, that this disillusioned view of the universe is most pervading and potent. The determined egoist has in all ages been hard for the moralist to handle. And now he can turn round on the moralist and invoke the universe to back him. The "struggle-for-lifeur" can plausibly maintain that it is he who in reality conforms to the fundamental law of all existence—that law being the self-preservation of each separate entity; and all alliances with other entities being mere temporary aids to self-preservation. "My ancestors," he may say, "instinctively practised tribal virtues, or they would not have survived. I can survive without practising those virtues; and if others imitate me, and my tribe decays, I shall merely infer that a nation containing many persons

above a certain pitch of intelligence must
necessarily lose the tribal instinct, the self-
sacrificing *naïveté*, which are essential to what
you call private virtue, or national greatness."
We may threaten to hold aloof from such a
man as this ; but he will reply that the society
of dupes or prigs is not the form of enjoyment
at which he particularly aims.

To all this, of course, the upright man has
for his own part an unshaken answer. He refuses to believe that the universe can be an
evil thing. Whatever his personal destiny may
be, he is ready to throw himself into the destiny of the whole. No disenchantment can
dislodge him from the august self-surrender of
Cleanthes' prayer :—

> Lead, lead Cleanthes, Zeus and holy Fate,
> Where'er ye place my post, to serve or wait :
> Willing I follow ; if against my will,
> A baffled rebel I must follow still.

To this temper the best men come nearest ;
this temper we should wish to be ours. And
yet we have no proof that it may not in very
truth be entirely irrational. The universe may
not expect anything of this kind, nor be prepared to meet our self-devotion in any way

whatever. All the moral grandeur which we
feel in the Cosmos may be the mere figment of
our own imaginations. This may be the last
form of man's ineradicable anthropomorphism ;
the ascription to the Sum of Things of that
merger of individual interests in a vaster well-
being which was necessary to our struggling
ancestors in order that their tribe might
survive.

The universe has no need to struggle for
existence ; it exists, and there is no more to
say. For aught we know, it may consist of
countless units of sensation, with no ultimate
end beyond their own individual and momentary pleasure, or surcease of pain, and only
linked into a semblance of community by the
exigencies of lust or war.

So profound is the atheism of these reflections,
that there is something repugnant even in the
admission that they need an answer. And yet
when, sometimes, an answer is hinted at by
some philosopher cognisant of the weakness of
the habitual positions, there is apt to be a
sinister tone in his reserve. It is suggested
that it need not always be deemed incumbent
on the moral teacher to proclaim that at all

hazards we must seek the truth.   If the wisest
men have decided that it is impossible to
" maintain Eternal Providence," it will be well
to say and think as little as possible about the
destiny of man.   Nay, it may be a duty to
preach to the young a lying gospel ; to hide
from them as long as may be the vanity of
human hope.   Science, it is urged, would thus
be only doing what religion has often done
before—setting a bar to inquiries which would
lead to demoralisation and despair.   Nor can
one say which would be the better justification :
the plea of religion, that she did but restrain
the soul from a risk of wilful and fatal error ;
or the plea which science would have to urge,
that she was but hiding the Medusa's head
under her robe, and keeping from men innocent
and unfortunate the inevitable and paralysing
truth.

For my own part, I am opposed to either
plea.   There seems to me to be something
even absurdly premature in this despair of
the human republic.   And, meantime, it is to
the simple, dispassionate love of truth, and to
this alone, that I can appeal in urging a line
of inquiry on which neither scientific nor

religious orthodoxy has thus far bestowed active support.

I maintain, then, that to suppose for a moment that mankind could have already arrived at any valid scientific conclusion nega- tiving our possible survival of death, is to show that the very idea that the subject can be treated scientifically has hardly yet entered men's minds. We sometimes see it said that " the highest intellects have grappled with the problem in vain for many an age." But what does this really mean? What materials have the highest intellects had to work upon? What observations have they made? What line of experiment have they pursued and found to be fruitless?

And what fraction of the probable duration on earth of the race of civilised men do such reasoners suppose to have already elapsed? Was there any abstract speculation worth speaking of five thousand years ago? And what proportion do five thousand years bear to the millions of years—place the number of millions as low as you will—during which, bar- ring accidents, we may suppose that the slowly- cooling sun will still be keeping our descendants

alive ?   Assuredly " we are ancients of the
earth and in the morning of the times," in a
sense far deeper than our habitual modes of
thought, our contrasts between " antiquity " and
the modern world, permit us to realise.   We
are still in the first moment of man's awakening
intelligence ; we are merely opening our eyes
upon the universe around us.

But even if we choose to speak of the past
duration of human thought as long, and of the
thinkers who have pondered on man's survival
as many in number, we may yet well ask
whether a failure thus far to solve any particular
problem need be taken as indicating that men
better equipped for the research will not solve
it in due time.   In dealing with any ordinary
branch of science such a question could have
but one answer.   The only reason why it is
needful here to press it is, that the existence or
nature of an unseen world around us has scarcely,
thus far, been treated as a scientific question
at all.

And yet, if an unseen world exists—and
supposing it to exist, we must in some sense
be in it—that world cannot consist only of
ideas and emotions, of theology and meta-

physics. It must be a world of science too, —a world governed by laws which cannot be moral laws alone, but which must regulate all that goes on in that world, and all communications (if any there be) which pass between that world and this.

The question, then, whether such communications can ever be received or understood, is in reality a question as to the possible extension of our terrestrial science so as to embrace possible indications of a life lying beyond, yet conceivably touching the life and the conditions of earth.

Now, the whole history of science is a history of the recognition and interpretation of continually slighter indications of forces or entities continually more subtle and remote. At each stage of progress there have been *savants* who have declared that the extreme limit of human perception had now been reached. At each stage observers accustomed to one set of inquiries, already easy and fruitful, have protested against new kinds of inquiry as chimerical and useless.

It happens thus, that an inquiry by positive methods into the survival of men, although, of

c

course, like other inquiries, it may be doomed
to ultimate failure, is, nevertheless, both an
almost new and a by no means hopeless thing.
So novel is it, that the very observations which
are urged most strongly *against* survival are
scarcely a generation old ; while the observations which tell *in favour* of survival have only
been systematically recorded within the last
decade.   Nor, in fact, need it surprise us that
the problem should have remained thus practically almost untouched.   The mere fact that a
problem is important to us is no reason why
we should expect that our ancestors should
have solved it.   The priest or the philosopher,
indeed, may give us answers on those matters
first which it most behoves us to know.   But
the *savant*, the actual observer and experimenter,
gives us answers first, not on the most important
problems, but on those which it is easiest to
solve.   We must discover the proper methods of
search before we can get at any given result.
Now, the proper methods in question touching
the intimate constitution of man — on which
constitution his survival or non-survival of death
must depend—are partly those of physiology
and partly those of psychology.   The methods

of physiology are new and imperfect ; the methods of experimental psychology are newer and more imperfect still.

As has been already implied, the scientific arguments *against* survival are themselves very recent. After that first obvious inference from the impenetrable silence of death, no further precision was given to the discussion until the middle of the present century. At about that date men began to realise the fact which John Stuart Mill could still treat as unproved— namely, that to every observable thought or emotion of man there probably corresponds some change or movement in the material sub- stance of the brain.

The exactness and delicacy with which these correspondences can now be established have made a deep impression on the public mind. We seem to have tracked mental life to its inmost recesses, and to have found it everywhere enwound with an organism which tells us much of our bestial origin, nothing of our spiritual future. The very pineal gland which Descartes suggested as the seat of the soul is now regarded as a degenerate vestige of the eye of an invertebrate ancestor.

And yet, however exactly the parallelism between psychical and cerebral energies may be established, the exacter correlation can tell us little more than the vaguer told us—little more than we had always known when noting the abeyance of the spiritual life in infancy, its distortion in madness, its decay in age.

No one, indeed, can now claim — but no one could ever reasonably claim—that the soul can sway and dominate the brain as it will, and express itself in its entirety through however defective an instrument. Going back to a metaphor as old as Plato, we know, even more surely than he did, that the musician cannot play sweetly on the lyre if it be strained or broken. But as to the origin or essential significance of this close connection of " psychosis and neurosis " we avowedly know nothing at all. We do not know whether the mental energy precedes or follows on the cerebral change, nor whether the two are, somehow, but different aspects of the same fact.

Thus far we are most of us agreed. We come now to a point of greater novelty. During the last few years experiments have been made, in France and in England, on the nature of human personality, which must influence our conception of this equation between mind and brain in directions as yet very imperfectly understood.

How quickly matters have moved may be best judged by a reference to the utterance of an advanced thinker a quarter of a century ago.

In 1865 the late John Stuart Mill, in his *Examination of Sir W. Hamilton's Philosophy*, had occasion to discuss the question whether "unconscious mental modifications" do or do not exist ; whether ideas can pass through the mind without forming a part, even for a moment, of the normal—assumed to be the only — current of consciousness. The only sentence which need here be cited from that discussion runs as follows : " The difference between the two opinions being *beyond the reach of experiment*" (the italics are mine), "and both being equally consistent with the facts which present themselves spontaneously, it is not easy to obtain sure grounds for deciding between them."

Most of my readers will be aware that it is, in fact, perfectly easy to decide this question by direct experiment in five minutes. Nay,

even at the date when Mill wrote, it was perfectly easy so to decide it, and the experiment
had been already made many thousands of
times ; so dangerous is it for even the greatest
philosophers to neglect even the humblest adit
into actual fact.

For, in truth, ever since the experiments, I
will not say of Mesmer, but of De Puységur, it
had been known to all those who were willing
to take the trouble to read a few books, and to
verify for themselves by actual trial the records
which those books contained — it had been
known, I say, that very many men and women
in normal health, could by various simple
methods be placed in the so-called somnambulic condition, or mesmeric trance, during
which state they could talk and act intelli-
gently ; but that when "awakened" from this
trance, they remembered absolutely nothing of
what had passed. It is as clear as such a
matter can reasonably be made,.that thoughts
and emotions of almost any degree of strength
and complexity may occupy a sane mind for
hours together, and yet at no time enter into
the current of ordinary waking consciousness.

This in itself is a striking fact enough, and

goes far to settle the question which Mill deemed incapable of direct attack. But these experiments have a significance which reaches far beyond the bounds of the ancient controversy. For the question is no longer of mere momentary intrusions into, or exclusions from, a stream of consciousness which is assumed to be practically synonymous with the man's entire being. On the contrary, we are now learning to conceive of our normal consciousness as representing only a fragment of the activity going on in our brains. We know of cases where a secondary current of consciousness — connected in various ways with the primary current—is always ready to take its place ; so that the person lives alternately two different lives, with different chains of memory, and even different characters. Nay, we know of cases, both spontaneous and experimentally induced, where the secondary consciousness has definitely replaced the primary one, and the person now possesses what would have been called in old times a different Self from that with which her earthly consciousness began.

These conclusions, I say, are now admitted ; but, although admitted, they are still, I think,

very imperfectly understood.   They have as
yet been observed mainly by physicians, who
have seldom realised their profound psychological meaning.   That meaning, as I understand it, is that no known form of human
consciousness manifests, or comes near to
manifesting, the total Self ; and, consequently,
that this empirical or superficial consciousness
with which we habitually identify ourselves
can only discover indirectly and inferentially,
by experiment and artifice, the extent of our
intellectual being.   We know not what fraction
of ourselves it may be which till now we have
taken for the whole.

As thus far stated, these expanding psychological prospects are still consistent with the
view that all our mental activities, however
extensive and however subdivisible, may be
dependent on cerebral changes, and may end
with death.   Yet even were there no new
powers visible in the widening inward horizon,
the very magnitude of the change in our conception of personality might well make us
pause before repeating the dogmas of negation
which were framed with regard to far simpler
and narrower facts.

Such a pause, at any rate, would soon
bring its own justification.   For in reality there
is much more to add.   Our notion of personality is being deepened as well as widened ; we
begin to discern profounder powers—powers
difficult to explain by any process of terrestrial
evolution, and indicating connections between
mind and mind of a character which there
seems no logical necessity that death should
interrupt or abolish.   The direct action of mind
upon mind at a distance, without the agency of
the recognised organs of sense, is a fact in
Nature (as I believe) which, although of frequent, or even of continual occurrence, can
rarely be so isolated and observed as to be
capable of direct and formal proof.   That it
has been, and is now being, so isolated and observed, under rigorous conditions, is the belief
of a growing group of experimenters in England
and other countries—a group which includes
not a few names already known for accurate
work accomplished in other fields.

Now this fact, as I deem it, of telepathy, or
the passage of thought and emotion from one
mind to another without sensory aid, does not
in itself carry obvious proof of anything in man

which the materialistic hypothesis might not
cover. "Brain-waves" might be a form of ether-
waves, or in some way analogous thereto ; and
this view, indeed, is now urged by the eminent
Italian *savant*, Professor Lombroso, who regards
telepathy as tending to show that thought is
essentially a vibratory energy, and possibly
capable of correlation with other modes of
motion. Assume the possibility of such a
view ; even thus, what need will there again be
of pause and readjustment ! But in truth even
the slight knowledge thus far gained of telepathy is enough to show something far more
complex than any single physical law can explain. When once we have got hold of this
transference of thoughts and images as an experimental fact, we find new analogies suggested,
and a new light thrown on many previously in-
explicable phenomena.

We find, for instance, that it is occasionally
possible for an experimenter to produce by
effort of will a hallucinatory image of himself
in the perception of a friend at a distance, without any previous suggestion or anticipation that
such an image would appear. This fact, of
which we have several instances, attested by

trustworthy persons at each end of the chain, forms a transition between ordinary experiments in thought-transference and those spontaneous hallucinatory images which occur so frequently at or about the moment of death, and represent the dying person to a distant friend, who is often not even aware of the illness. These " Phantasms of the Living," again, although they may not actually prove that man is other than a purely material being, do at any rate so extend and alter our conception of his hidden powers that our previous psychology is seen to need fundamental readjustment. Nay more ; the connection of these apparitions with the *unconscious self* is significant in the extreme. It appears that the projection of a phantom of this kind, although it sometimes follows on an exertion of conscious will, is much more frequently an unconscious act, and takes place while the " agent " or person whose image is projected is asleep, or fainting, or even in the comatose condition which often precedes death. Now this projection of a phantom into other minds is a psychical activity of some kind, and some cerebral activity must, I do not doubt, correspond with it. But whatever the equation thus implied may be, it assuredly must contain some elements which are not allowed for in the formulæ by which the concomitance between "psychosis and neurosis" is commonly expressed. We generally suppose, for instance, that a rapid flow of blood through the brain is necessary for vigorous pyschical action. But in some of our published cases the dying man seems to produce a strong psychical effect at a distance while he is lying in a state of coma, with bodily functions at their lowest ebb. In short, this kind of special telepathic energy seems to vary inversely, rather than directly, with the observable activity of the nervous system or of the conscious mind.

The solution of this puzzle is not likely to be found without a far wider knowledge of actual facts than we have yet attained. It is encouraging, therefore, to observe that the scientific world is gradually beginning to realise the importance of collecting and analysing all those instructive psychological phenomena which we class under the title of *hallucinations*, since, whatever of truth their purport may contain, they possess at any rate the special hallucinatory quality of suggesting

some material object which is not actually
present. The International Congress of Experimental Psychology, which was opened in
Paris in 1889 by the well-known psychologist
M. Ribot, undertook the continuance of a
Census of Hallucinations, which had been
already set on foot, and which has since been
carried on in France by M. Marillier, in
America by Professor William James of Har-
vard, and in England by Professor Sidgwick of
Cambridge. The object of this inquiry—which,
be it observed, is not mystical but statistical—is
to determine what percentage of sane and healthy
persons experience hallucinations of any kind,
what the nature or causes of such hallucinations
appear to be, and what percentage of them are
truth-telling, or veridical—coincide, that is to
say, with some actual fact at a distance not
otherwise known, as when a man sees the figure
of a friend who dies at that moment.[1]

This whole quest, it should be understood, is
practically a new one. Hallucinations had, of
course, been already studied (though in somewhat cursory fashion) as symptoms of disease.

[1] The Report of the Census is expected to appear this year
(1893) as Part XXV. of the *Proceedings of the Society for
Psychical Research* (Kegan Paul, Trench, Trübner, and Co.)

And of late years the induction of hallucination in sane and healthy persons during the hypnotic trance had begun to be recognised as an experimental method of great value in psychology. But comparatively few *savants* have yet realised the extreme variety and instructiveness of the phantasmal sights and sounds which occur spontaneously to normal persons, and which it is now for the first time becoming possible to study in a systematic instead of a merely anecdotic manner.

And here we, of course, come face to face with the question whether any of these phantasmal appearances, which we hold to give frequent evidence of an influence of living men at a distance, can be held to give evidence of an influence of the still remoter dead. The first thing needed in such an inquiry has been to set aside altogether, not only the mass of ill - attested stories on which the believer in ghosts has been wont to rely, but also the very grounds of belief to which such stories have mainly appealed. It cannot be admitted that if, say, a mourning husband sees the phantasmal figure of his deceased wife, and hears her speak, there is proof of anything beyond a mere sub-

jective affection.   No emotional fitness, no mere
vividness of perception, can prove that the figure
was not generated by the percipient's own
brooding memories.   But if the supposed
husband does not know that his wife is dead,
or even ill, and yet sees her figure shortly after
her death, the apparition at once acquires
evidential value.   And if, not a mourning
husband, but some complete stranger, sees a
phantasmal figure, and afterwards identifies
that figure amongst a number of photographs,
and it turns out to represent someone who has
recently died in the room where the apparition
was seen — then, again, we have a kind of
coincidence which, if often repeated, must
indicate something more than chance, although
the precise meaning of the incident may still be
far from clear.   Again, if several persons simul-
taneously or successively (but independently of
each other) see a phantasmal figure which they
describe in similar terms, it seems probable that
some cause is at work beyond the mere subjective state of the percipients in question.

The study of cases of this type (many of
which I have set forth elsewhere) has gradually
convinced me that the least improbable hypo-

thesis lies in the supposition that some influence
on the minds of men on earth is occasionally
exercised by the surviving personalities of men
departed.   I believe this influence to be, usually,
of an indirect and dreamlike character, but I
cannot explain the facts to myself without
supposing that such an influence exists.

I am further strengthened in this belief by the
study of the automatic phenomena briefly noticed
above.   I observe that in all the varieties of
automatic action—of which automatic writing
may be taken as a prominent type—the contents
of the messages given seem to be derived from
three sources.   First of all comes the automatist's
own mind.   From that the vast bulk of the
messages are undoubtedly drawn, even when
they refer to matters which the automatist once
knew, but has entirely forgotten.   Whatever
has gone into the mind may come out of the
mind ; although this automatism may be the
only way of getting at it.   Secondly, there is
a small percentage of messages apparently
telepathic—containing, that is to say, facts
probably unknown to the automatist, but
known to some living person in his company,
or connected with him.   But, thirdly, there is

a still smaller residuum of messages which I cannot thus explain—messages which contain facts apparently not known to the automatist nor to any living friend of his, but known to some deceased person, perhaps a total stranger to the living man whose hand is writing. I cannot avoid the conviction that in some way —however dreamlike and indirect—it is the departed personality which originates such messages as these.[1]

I by no means wish to impose these views upon minds not prepared to accept them. What I do desire is, that as many other men as possible should qualify themselves to judge independently of the value of the evidence on which I rely—should study what has been collected, and should repeat the experiments and extend the observations which are essential to the formation of any judgments worth the name.

To those who have watched with personal interest the slow stages which had to be passed through before the simpler facts of hypnotism received official recognition as facts and not as

---

[1] See *Proceedings of the Society for Psychical Research*, Part XVI., etc.

frauds, the gradual pace at which these more
advanced phenomena are finding acceptance is
in no way surprising. The general public are
little aware of the persistent disregard of good
evidence, as well as of bad, with which the
early school of mesmerists were met by the
medical world of their day. Yet the study of
that slow victory over prejudice and apathy
forms one of the most instructive chapters in
the history of science.

Gradually one phenomenon after another of
those discovered and attested by De Puységur,
Esdaile, Elliotson, etc., has been admitted into
orthodox science under some slightly altered
name. Certain phenomena, rarer and more
difficult to examine, but attested by the same
men with equal care, are still left in the outer
court of the scientific temple. But when one
has seen the somnambulic state, the insensibility
under operations, etc., which were once scouted
as fraudulent nonsense, becoming the common-
places of the lecture-room, one can await with
equanimity the general acceptance of the
thought - transference and the clairvoyance
which, from De Puységur's day onwards, have
repeatedly occurred in the course of those same

experiments — experiments which sometimes
ruined the careers of those who made them,
but which are now recognised as epoch-
making in a great department of experimental
psychology.

I place together then—as I claim that history gives me a *primâ facie* right to do—
certain experiments which have, so to say,
gained general acceptance but yesterday, and
certain cognate experiments which are on their
way (as I think) to general acceptance on
some not distant morrow ; and I draw from
these a double line of argument in favour of
human survival. In the first place, I point
to the great extension and deepening which
experiment has given to our conception of the
content and capacities of the sub-conscious
human mind,—amounting, perhaps, to a shifting
of man's psychical centre of gravity from the
conscious to the sub-conscious or subliminal
strata of his being—and accompanied by the
manifestation of powers at least not obviously
derivable from terrestrial evolution.

And, in the second place, I claim that there
is, in fact, direct evidence for the exercise of
some kind of influence by the surviving per-

sonalities of departed men. I claim that the analysis of phantasmal sights and sounds, treated by careful rules of evidence, indicates this influence. And I claim that it is indicated also by the analysis of those automatic messages which, in various manners, carry upwards to the threshold of consciousness the knowledge acquired from unknown sources by the sub-conscious mind.

And now a word as to the special character of the fragments of knowledge as to things unseen which I regard as having been reached in the aforesaid manner. The only claim which I make for this knowledge is a claim considerably humbler than prophet or preacher has usually advanced. I do not say that these are such facts as might be selected from the whole universe of facts to edify or to console us. But I say that they are such facts as we should have been likely, on any scientific method, to get hold of amongst the first, and to assimilate the most easily.

If there be an invisible universe, it will be easiest for us to imagine it after the analogy of the largest conception which we apply to the visible universe. We shall accordingly con-

ceive it as an immense, coherent process of
evolution, in which Thought and Consciousness
are not, as the materialists hold them, a mere
epiphenomenon, an accidental and transitory
accompaniment of more permanent energies, a
light that flashes out from the furnace door but
does none of the work,—but, on the other hand,
are, and always have been, the central subject
of the evolutionary process itself.

Now, if this be the case, we should expect
that our first intimation of the true extra-
terrene character of our evolution might be the
accidental discovery of some faculty within us
which was not traceable to the action of our
terrene antecedents. Here, as elsewhere, we
might expect that knowledge of the future
might be attained by inference from the past.
The comparison of man as he is to the caterpillar, and of man as he may be after death to
the butterfly, is a tolerably old one. Let
us suppose that some humble larvæ are
dissecting each other, and speculating as to
their destinies. At first they find themselves
precisely suited to life and death on a cabbage-
leaf. Then they begin to observe certain points
in their construction which are useless to larval

life.   These are, in fact, what are called
" imaginal   characters " — points   of   structure
which indicate that the larva has descended
from an imago, or perfect insect, and is destined
in his turn to become one himself.   These
characters are much overlaid by the secondary
or larval characters, which subserve larval, and
not imaginal life, and they consequently may
easily be overlooked or ignored.   But our supposed caterpillar sticks to his point ; he maintains that these characteristics indicate an aerial
origin.   And now a butterfly settles for a
moment on the cabbage-leaf.   The caterpillar
points triumphantly to the morphological iden-
tity of some of the butterfly's conspicuous
characters with some of his own latent characters ; and while he is trying to persuade his
fellow-caterpillars of this, the butterfly flies
away.

    This is exactly what I hold to have hap-
pened in the history of human evolution.   I
will mention one or two great names alone.
Plato was the first larva to insist upon the
imaginal characters.   His doctrine of Reminiscence asserted that our quasi-instinctive recognition of geometrical truths, etc., implied that

we, in fact, *remembered* these truths ; that geometrical capacity was a character carried into
this world with us from some other stage of
being.   And the view thus pressed by Socrates
and Plato, the very founders of science, is now
renewed by the foremost of living naturalists.
Mr. Wallace holds, as is well known, a modifi-
cation of Plato's view.   He considers that these
sudden increments of faculty—mathematical,
musical, and the like—which occur without
apparent hereditary cause, indicate some access
of energy outside the order of purely terrene
evolution.   Somewhat similarly, I would suggest that telepathy and cognate faculties now
beginning to be recognised as inherent in the
sub-conscious strata of the human intelligence,
may be the results of an evolution other than
that terrene or physical evolution whose successive steps and slowly-growing capacities we
can in some rough way retrace.

Yet one more point to complete the parallel
which I have suggested between the man and
the caterpillar.   We have discovered (as I hold)
that we men can occasionally communicate
among ourselves in a fashion at once inexplic-
able and practically useless—a fashion for

which no origin suggests itself in the history of
terrene evolution. And we observe also, that
information not attainable by ordinary methods
is sometimes conveyed to us by this method. I
argue, as the caterpillar argued about the
butterfly, that here is a similarity of structure
between our own intelligence and some unseen
intelligence, and that what that unseen intelligence is we too may once have been, and may
be destined again to be. And, addressing myself for a moment to the religious and philosophical side of man, I point out that our small
or even grotesque cases of telepathic trans-
mission between living men, or between the
men called living and the men called dead,
stand towards certain of the central beliefs of
the Gospels and of some high philosophies in
the same relation in which laboratory experiments stand to the vast operations of Nature.
That same direct influence of mind on mind
which we show *in minimis* would, if supposed
operative *in maximis*, be a form of stating the
efficacy of prayer, the communion of saints, or
even the operation of a Divine Spirit.

To those who will say that all this is a mere
fantasy played on the great theme of Evolution,

I would suggest that the theory of Evolution can never be—I do not say complete—but even coherent, until it can say some plausible word on Life, Consciousness, Thought ; and that even inconclusive experiments—if ours are inconclusive—and misinterpreted observations—if ours are misinterpreted—may be the inevitable pathway through which the human mind gropes onwards into fuller light.   And to those, on the other hand, who disdain the paltriness, the unspiritual character of our results, and who would fain keep alive the religious glow in humanity with no definite basis of proof, I would reply, that by small accretions sure foothold may be upbuilt, and that he who stands on a narrow coral island in mist and night will in the end see more than he who floats dreamily amid the splendours of sunset which illumine an ever-shadowing sea.

But, indeed, whatever be the significance of the facts which in my own view are already established, I am anxious not to claim from my readers more than they can fairly concede.   I do not claim that all men ought to be convinced ; but only that men whose minds are free from prepossession ought to feel that there is a case for further inquiry. Nor can we even assume that the minds, even of able and honest men, will, in fact, be free from prepossession in such a matter as this. Most men of middle age have formed some decided opinion on points so vital ; and they must for some time continue, I do not say to judge the new evidence in the light of the old opinion, but to retain the old opinion, whatever they may think of the new evidence. I have met with instances on both sides. I know certain agnostic *savants* whose intellect pronounces the new evidence to be very strong, but whose habitual temper of mind does not permit them to dwell upon the conclusions to which that evidence points. And, on the other hand, I know certain theologians and metaphysicians who take for granted, without examination, that the new evidence must needs break down, and the new researches come to nothing, but who nevertheless continue to treat man's immortality as already proved to demonstration by favourite arguments of their own.

Such men as these—and many of our best minds are among them—will never seriously grapple with a new and complex inquiry which lies far outside their habitual line of thought. We must appeal—as is commonly the case in any new departure of great moment—to a somewhat younger generation. There are many men now entering on active intellectual life who are practically devoid of any prepossession; who feel neither the old religious fervour, nor, on the other hand, that ardour of negation which formed the brief reaction from an orthodox domination which could no longer maintain its hold. Such men believe in the methods of science, and in little else; but they are often animated by a deep sympathy for mankind, and are impelled to a practical benevolence which would fain base itself upon a larger hope.

It is these men whom I wish to convince, not that my own answer to any given problem is the true one, but simply and solely that these most momentous problems of human fate can be, and must be, attacked with precisely the same steady care and dispassionate candour as have been already employed upon those myriad problems on which science has established a "consensus of experts," and has set mankind at unity.

The time for *a priori* chains of argument,

for the subjective pronouncements of leading
minds, for amateurish talk and pious opinion,
has passed away; the question of the survival
of man is a branch of Experimental Psychology.
Is there, or is there not, evidence in the actual
observed phenomena of automatism, apparitions,
and the like, for a transcendental energy in
living men, or for an influence emanating from
personalities which have overpassed the tomb?
This is the definite question, which we can at
least intelligibly discuss, and which either we
or our descendants may some day hope to
answer.

And what, after all, is this appeal of mine
except a last assertion of the inductive method
in a field from which Bacon debarred that
method only because he deemed the position
already impregnable without need of further
proof? You may say, of course, that the
evidence which has thus far been collected, by
a few men, in a few years, is weak and insufficient. You may say this, I repeat, either
after perusing the dozen or so of necessary
volumes, or, as is more usual, without thinking
it needful to study the actual facts at all. But
in this age of the world you can scarcely impugn

the temper of mind which prompts the inquiry ;
the readiness to repeat minute experiments, to
analyse obscure indications, to prefer small facts
to great assumptions—in short, what Bacon
calls " the true and legitimate humiliation of the
human spirit." And when Bacon speaks of
those who " have but cast a glance or two upon
facts and examples and experience, and straight-
way proceeded, as if invention were nothing
more than an exercise of thought, to invoke
their own spirits to give them oracles," are we
not reminded of many a proud conclusion of
the metaphysician who would by his own mere
sign-manual renounce the heritage of the race ;
—of many an "*ignoramus et ignorabimus*" of
the *savant* who would fain set his own private
boundary to the still-advancing tide-wave of the
discoveries and the dominion of man ?

What other effort after knowledge is equally
worth our pains ? What possibility lies before
mankind of equal magnitude with this possibility
of demonstrating the existence of an unseen
world, and man's communication therewith or
existence therein ? We are standing, be it remembered, at the very beginning of the probable
period of civilised human habitation of this

planet. We live in the infancy of our race ;
but we have not the child's boundless expect-
ation of knowledge or of joy.   On the contrary,
the necessary limits of our material science are
dimly divined, at a distance which men already
begin to measure, albeit with that calmness
with which we regard the possible troubles of a
hundredth generation.   If we allow ourselves a
speculation so perilously remote, we have to admit that the nature of light itself, the structure
of our own sense-organs, the character of the
elements of which our planet is composed, all
indicate that there are boundaries of observation
which no instruments and no inferences can
overpass, and that after a few more thousand
years, if you will, of theoretic discovery, we
shall be reduced to mere practical applications
of such small fraction of the facts of the universe
as have proved accessible to men who can but
peer through the bars of a prison-house into an
illimitable world.

On the moral side, moreover, as well as on
the scientific, we know what limitations of the
ideal are imposed by the narrowing of our prospect to earth alone.   I shall not here enter on
the question of the intrinsic value of human

life, if that life ends in the tomb.   It is enough
to say that in the very Utopias framed by so-
called Secular or Positivist enthusiasm, the
elements of enterprise and aspiration—the
" high strife and glorious hazard " of which Plato
speaks—avowedly and inevitably tend to disappear.   Suppose, for instance, an entirely successful Socialism—suppose the earth inhabited
by a fixed number of healthy persons, living in
equal luxury and universal peace.   What are
these men and women to think of or to look to
more? or what will be left *Epicuri de grege porcis*
to give to life its mystery, its hope, its charm?
Now I do not say that the consideration of the
salutary results of any given belief should lead
us to entertain that belief on insufficient
evidence.   But I do say that such prospect of
consequences should urge to strenuous effort
along lines of inquiry which can be so straight-
forwardly conducted, so strictly defined, that it
shall be open to all to criticise the process
and to estimate the result.   " If in anything,"
says Bacon again, " I have been either too cred-
ulous or too little awake and attentive, or if I
have fallen off by the way, and left the inquiry
incomplete, nevertheless, I so present these

things naked and open that my errors can be
marked and set aside before the mass of knowledge be further infected by them ; and it will
be easy also for others to continue and carry
on my labours." Such, surely, is the temper in
which those should work who hold that this
same patient subjection of the human spirit to
the facts of the universe, this same obedience to
Nature—whom we hope in the end to rule—
may at last extend beyond the material Cosmos
the prospect and the hopes of man.

I will conclude this paper with a curious
illustration of that survival of mediæval conceptions which prevents men from approaching
this problem with a clear and open mind. The
effort to prove that there is a life beyond the
grave is sometimes spoken of as *selfish*, by the
very men who declare themselves most eager to
promote the terrestrial welfare of their fellows.
It is hard to say why it should be philanthropic to
desire the lesser boon for mankind, and selfish
to desire the greater ; unless, indeed, the genuine philanthropist is forbidden to aim at any
common benefit in which he himself may expect
to share. In reality, this confusion of mind has
a deeper source ; it is a vestige of the old monk-

ish belief that man's welfare in the next world
was something in itself idle and personal, and
was to be attained by means inconsistent with
man's welfare in *this*.   Whether Christianity
ever authorised such a notion I do not now in-
quire.   It is certain, at any rate, that Science
will never authorise it.   We are making as safe
a deduction from world-wide analogy as man
can ever make regarding things thus unknown
when we assume that spiritual evolution will
follow the same laws as physical evolution ;
that there will be no discontinuity between
terrene and post-terrene bliss or virtue, and
that the next life, like this, will " resemble
wrestling rather than dancing," and will find
its best delight in the possibllity of progress,
not attainable without effort so strenuous as
may well resemble pain.

There will, no doubt, in such a quest, be an
element of personal hope as well ; but man,
after all, must desire something, and what
better can he desire ?   There is little danger, I
think, that with eyes fixed on so great a
prospect, he should sink into a self-absorption
which forgets his kind.   Rather, perhaps, the
race of man itself may sometimes seem to him

but a little thing in comparison with the majesty of that spiritual universe into whose intimate structure it may thus, and thus only, be possible to project one penetrating ray. Yet we ourselves are a part, not only of the race, but of the universe. It is conceivable that our share in its fortunes may be more abiding than we know ; that our evolution may be not planetary but cosmical, and our destiny without an end. *Major agit deus, atque opera in majora remittit.*

CHARLES DARWIN AND
AGNOSTICISM

Unde refert nobis victor, quid possit oriri,
Quid nequeat ; finita potestas denique cuique
Quanam sit ratione, atque alte terminus hærens.
LUCRETIUS.

WE cannot doubt upon what man in our own
day the Roman iconoclast would have bestowed
the famous eulogy from which these lines are
drawn. To prove what can arise and what
cannot ; to show the predetermined potency of
every life, and the bound firm-fixed by Fate ;
—all this was the privilege of Charles Darwin
as it never has been of any other. No one
other man by his own mere tranquil observation
and thought has ever modified so profoundly
the common creed of mankind. No one, as
Lucretius would have put it, has ever so scattered
the night of superstition by "lucid shafts of

day." But the strange thing is that in this single instance Lucretius and the Pontifical College should, so to say, have been at one ; that the sanctuary of the prophet of an old ideal should have been opened to the prophet of a new, and that Darwin should be laid in the shrine of Peter.

His reception therein was deeply and honourably significant—significant of a resolute national candour which, when the case is proved and the first shock over, will set no dogma higher than truth. And it was significant also of the continuity between the two ideals, of the fact that virtue and duty are in essentials the same to the man who treats this life as all as to the man " begotten again unto a lively hope by the resurrection of Jesus Christ from the dead." For the personal character of the great innovator largely influenced the reception of his teaching by the mass of mankind. Insensibly that character, in spite of all his retirement, had stolen upon the world, through letters, through interviews, even through the tone of his scientific treatises, and from the *Life and Letters*, now before us, we do but fill the details into an outline which was already known. For the biographer's task one thing was needful—a deep hereditary congruity of temper, an attitude towards Darwin such as was Darwin's towards Nature, the unobtrusive and sagacious interpretation of an object of reverence and love. As it has here been told, the life unfolds itself like a pure process of growth and fruitage, and needs defence or eulogy no more than a tree or a flower.

Besides the picture of Darwin's private life and the mass of letters illustrative of the development of his ideas, the book contains a few pages which briefly answer the question which many have wished to ask, namely, What was Darwin's own view of the light thrown by the evolution theory and by his own work therein upon the old problems of the soul and Providence, the intimate nature and the ultimate destiny of man? His weighty words afford material for much thought; and the few reflections which here follow are not intended either to defend or to assail the agnostic position which he takes up, but rather to indicate certain channels into which the time-honoured controversies at present tend to flow.

Four points may be briefly touched upon;

firstly, the weakening effect of Darwinism on
the argument for Providence drawn from the
consensus of mankind ; secondly, its weakening
effect on a similar argument drawn from the
sense of sin and forgiveness ; thirdly, its apparent incompatibility with the creationist
theory of the genesis of the human soul ; and
fourthly, the still more urgent question whether,
if agnosticism, in default of fresh evidence to
an unseen world, becomes the prevalent attitude
of men's minds, we may suppose that our
posterity will acquiesce with Darwin's cheerfulness in the abandonment of the ancient hope.

(1) " In my journal," says Darwin in 1876 [*Life*, i.
311], " I wrote that whilst standing in the midst of the
grandeur of a Brazilian forest, ' it is not possible to give
an adequate idea of the higher feelings of wonder,
admiration, and devotion which fill and elevate the
mind.'   I well remember my conviction that there is
more in man than the mere breath of his body.   But
now the grandest scenes would not cause any such
convictions and feelings to rise in my mind.   It may
be truly said that I am like a man who has become
colour-blind, and the universal belief by men of the
existence of redness makes my present loss of perception of not the least value as evidence.   This
argument would be a valid one if all men of all races
had the same inward conviction of the existence of
one God ; but we know that this is very far from

being the case." And again [i. 313], "Then arises the doubt, Can the mind of man, which has, as I fully believe, been developed from a mind as low as that possessed by the lowest animal, be trusted when it draws such grand conclusions? . . . Would any one trust in the convictions of a monkey's mind, if there are any convictions in such a mind?"

It will be seen that the difficulty is twofold. In the first place, if we are compelled to recognise our ancestors as lower beings than ourselves, the tradition of antiquity becomes, so to say, worse than nothing ; and in the second place, however greatly we may have advanced upon our ancestors, if nevertheless all our beliefs and emotions have been derived from theirs by slow continuous development, we cannot well have acquired a new and direct knowledge as to a matter to which our senses bear no evidence. Mr. Wallace, as is well known, conjectures that some influence, resembling that of man on the domestic animals, may have been brought to bear upon primitive man "during that strange intermediate period during which he was passing from brute to man," and that some power of spiritual communion, differentiating man from the lower races, may have been thus originated. This view has not found many adherents ; yet I cannot discover what is the actual hypothesis generally framed by those who hold that there is in fact " some difference in kind and in spiritual nature between man and brute." The evolution theory, however, almost compels us to make our notions on this point in some way definite, if we are to attribute more weight to the religious instincts of saints and sages than to " the convictions of a monkey's mind."

(2) Our next topic is the change which the evolution theory—especially as expounded in chapter iii. of the *Descent of Man*—has introduced into our conception of *sin*. In the old view, the sense of sin involved a sense of relationship with a Power above ourselves whom we had offended, but who might also forgive us. Too often, in earlier ages, the sinner conceived his offence to be unpardonable, and was " thrust," as Article XVII. has it, " either into desperation, or into wretchlessness of most unclean living, no less perilous than desperation." Here, then, especially might Lucretius have hailed Darwin as a *liberator* of mankind. For on the theory of descent, our sense of sin is a sense of relation, not to a

higher Power, but to our own remote and savage progenitors. If I commit a selfish or violent act, this is because the impulse to immediate enjoyment, or to self-defence, which I inherit from half-human ancestors, is temporarily stronger than the impulse to self-control or to forgiveness, which my more recent ancestors have slowly acquired and imperfectly transmitted. The remorse which follows on my action is due to the fact that the impulse which I have outraged is permanent in my breast, whilst the impulse which I have gratified was a fleeting one, and has expired with its gratification. My sin, then, so far as it went, was a case of reversion, of arrested development ; it does not justify " desperation," or suggest the infinite anger of offended Deity. Yet, on the other hand, in losing the sense of divine offence we lose the sense of divine aid, of divine forgiveness. If we feel that there is no access by which spiritual strength may be borne upon the soul, and if we are at the same time conscious of helpless weakness, our new state is surely a bondage rather than a liberation— a bondage to the inexorable laws of heredity, which have determined at our birth that we shall be able to struggle thus far, and no farther, along the upward way.

Or shall we say that while the young child is praised or blamed by its mother for every act, a school is chosen for the boy, and he is sent there to shift for himself till the holidays come? "I cannot, anyhow, be contented," says Darwin in 1860 (ii. 312), "to view this wonderful universe, and especially the nature of man, and to conclude that everything is the result of brute force. I am inclined to look at everything as resulting from designed laws, with the details, whether good or bad, left to the working out of what we may call chance."

Shall we suppose, then, that in the sight of some higher Power our battles in this small world are not, after all, very tremendous, and that we are all the better for being left to fight them out by ourselves? Or shall we ever learn more of some transcendent communication? of influences falling upon our spirit from behind the veil of visible things?

(3) Passing from these problems drawn from our actual earthly descent to the realm of philosophical, or perhaps I should rather say theological, speculation, it seems worth observ-

ing that the whole evolution theory, and
Darwin's work in particular, has given to one
among several theories of the genesis of
the soul a certain analogical advantage over
its ancient rivals. Those thinkers who have
assumed that man possesses a *soul*, in the sense
of some individualised vital principle surviving
the death of the body, have naturally speculated
as to the soul's origin, and the mode in which
it joins connection with the body. *Creationists*
have supposed that a soul was created by a
fresh act of God for each new body. *Tradu-
cianists* have maintained that the soul was
engendered by the parents, and transmitted like
the bodily characteristics. *Infusionists* have
held that the soul pre-existed elsewhere, but
was infused into the body at some given
moment. And *Transmigrationists*, developing
this last doctrine, have held that the soul, thus
infused into man, had previously inhabited the
bodies of other men or animals.

These speculations, which occupied many
great minds in the past, have now an air of
fantastic unreality. Yet the unfamiliarity of
the ordinary church-goer with such hypotheses
by no means necessarily implies that he has

risen above them.   Very probably he is content with a crude form of the Creationist
hypothesis, without much regard either to the
difficulties which old theology found in it or
to those which modern science suggests.   Its
main difficulty in the schoolmen's eyes (and
this Traducianism strove to meet) lay in the
existence of "original sin."   It was hard to
believe that a soul so imperfect as ours came
fresh from the hand of the Creator.   And the
scientific objection would be of a parallel kind.
Just as it is impossible to suppose that our
bodies, with their vestigial organs and their
embryonic history, can be the results of a single
creative impulse, even of a single creative
impulse communicated to the race to which
they belong, so also is it impossible to suppose
that the similarly complex, similarly imperfect
psychical element in us, if veritably separable
from the corporeal, can be the result of one
isolated creative impulse, given at some definite
moment for each individual.

Yet surely, if we are to talk about the soul
at all, we dare not altogether decline to search
for some conceivable hypothesis of its origin-
ation.   Is Traducianism conceivable?   Can we

give any meaning to the notion of direct psychical progeniture from father to son?   Are we not driven back on some form of Transmigrationism? some notion at least so far parallel with evolutionary theory as to allow us to think of the soul as in some way pre-existent—as having in some way undergone a progressive development analogous to the hereditary development which has made our bodies what they are?   And may we not still see some reason in Plato's method, in his attempt to throw light on the soul's present and her future by collecting what seemed to him the traces of her existence in the past?   His doctrine of *reminiscence* may have been but a rough scaffolding for such inquiry, yet was he not after all well inspired in thus looking for what we should now call the intellectual or emotional *vestiges* of a life passed under other conditions than ours, or, say, indications of descent from some winged creature which our "larval characters" do not wholly hide?

(4) This last speculation, though showing to what distant fields of thought the influence of the evolution theory extends, is, I need hardly say, nowhere noticed by Darwin himself.

Absolutely open to every kind of definite
evidence, his mind refuses to dwell for long on
shadowy possibilities.   Where testimony seems
to him inadequate, and not capable of fresh
reinforcement, it insensibly fades from his view.
In a characteristic passage [i. 308] he describes
the mode in which he underwent that gradual
loss of Christian belief which has come to
many minds with such storms of emotion, such
unreasoning alternations of hope and fear.

I was very unwilling to give up my belief.   I feel
sure of this, for I can well remember often and often
inventing day-dreams of old letters between distinguished Romans, and manuscripts being discovered at
Pompeii or elsewhere, which confirmed in the most
striking manner all that was written in the Gospels.
But I found it more and more difficult, with free
scope given to my imagination, to invent evidence
which would suffice to convince me.   Thus disbelief
crept over me at a very slow rate, but was at last
complete.   The rate was so slow that I felt no
distress.

Darwin, it will be seen, began with what
would be called a quite healthy and normal
instinct of reverence and faith.   Then gradually
this disappears without a struggle ; it is not
ejected from the system (as, say, with Mr.
Froude) ; it is not *encysted* (as, say, with J. S.

Mill) ; it is simply *atrophied*, and dissolves pain-
lessly away ; and the loss seems to leave no
sense as of a void encompassing.   He does not
(to vary the metaphor) make his own definite
facts stand out from a dusky background of the
Absolute and the Unknowable, but when anywhere he finds evidence failing him he simply
says, " We cannot tell."

Again, while he is quite ready to publish
unpopular opinions, if candour requires it (as in
the case of the *Descent of Man*), his agnosticism is
far too modest and gentle-hearted to allow him
to feel the mere joy of combat, the impulse
which makes a man willing to admit that he
knows nothing himself for the pleasure of
proving to men who think they know more
that they know in fact, if possible, less.   It
has been fortunate for the intellectual interest
of life that the peace-loving Darwin and the
self-effacing Wallace should have had a coad-
jutor more vividly touched with earthly fire, like
the mortal charger who, champing more fiercely
in the battle's fray, kept pace with the two
undying steeds of Achilles.   But we must
remember that Professor Huxley's trenchant
polemic has cast a kind of glory about the

mere fact of man's ignorance which cannot
possibly be kept up for long.   Battles there
will always be ; but never again, perhaps, such
a plunging through half-armed foemen, such an
ἀριστεία of the Agnostic as we associate with
that brilliant name.

Once more : it is characteristic of Darwin's
sobriety of mind that, although he does not
pretend personally to regret old faiths, he does
not throw the slightest optimistic colouring
around his novel conceptions.   A tone of
triumph comes readily to a man who feels that
he is upsetting error and preaching truth ; and
this tone is sometimes taken when it is strangely
inappropriate to the actual bearing of the message thus proclaimed.   If there be no God, and
we perish for ever, it may be right to say so and
to face the facts as best one can ; but one must
indeed be optimistic to find much to be *pleased*
at.   This optimistic illusion, which Mr. Frederic
Harrison, for instance, so eloquently maintains,
seems to spring partly from the mere joy of
battle already spoken of, and partly from an
instinct, lingering on from the ages of faith, that,
be it what it may, the order of the Universe
must be good.   " Why good ?   Why better

than the very worst?" the gathering band of
pessimists call from every side; and Darwin
[i. 309] goes perhaps as far as wary science
will allow when he points out that the mere
influence of natural selection guarantees a
certain amount of happiness in the races that
survive, inasmuch as "if all the individuals of
any species were habitually to suffer to an
extreme degree they would neglect to propagate
their kind; but we have no reason to believe
that this has ever, or at least often, occurred."

Thus much for the present of mankind;
while as to its future some words of Darwin's
are here given [i. 3 1 2], which, considering his
cautious temper, are perhaps as noteworthy as
any which ever fell from his pen. For he deals
here with the very remotest events which we
have any definite warrant for predicting, with
that eschatology with which science has replaced
the second advent and the millennial reign.

With respect to immortality, nothing shows me
so clearly how strong and almost instinctive a belief
it is, as the consideration of the view now held by most
physicists, namely, that the sun with all the planets will
in time grow too cold for life, unless indeed some
great body dashes into the sun, and thus gives it fresh
life. Believing as I do that man in the distant future

F

will be a far more perfect creature than he now is, it is an intolerable thought that he and all other sentient beings are doomed to complete annihilation after such long-continued slow progress. To those who fully admit the immortality of the human soul, the destruction of our world will not appear so dreadful.

Amidst the calm advance of Darwin's armies of scientific facts against the old creeds of men, this expression of " an intolerable thought" comes to us like the cry of Scipio Aemilianus over burning Carthage, when the ruin which his own legions had wrought suggested to him that Rome herself must some day fall.

> Ἔσσεται ἦμαρ ὅτ᾽ ἄν ποτ᾽ ὀλώλῃ Ἴλιος ἱρὴ
> καὶ Πρίαμος καὶ λαὸς ἐϋμμελίω Πριάμοιο.

On the whole, therefore, in reviewing Darwin's life, we find neither any prejudice which warps his reception of evidence of any kind, nor any emotional pre-occupation which interferes with steady and fruitful labour upon the facts before him.   In the old phrase of Sir T. Browne, he " swims smoothly in the stream of his nature, and lives but one man."   He seems, as already said, to be the exemplar of a new ideal, a man as well adapted to human life, on the hypothesis that this earth is all that we can know, as a John or a Paul was adapted to human life on the hypothesis that our citizenship is in heaven.

How, then, we ask ourselves, does the new ideal bear comparison with the old as regards the virtue or the happiness which that old ideal aimed at securing?

On the moral side there is certainly no perceptible decline. Never, perhaps, did a biography give such an unmixedly pleasing impression both of its hero and of his friends. In these hundreds of unstudied letters there is not a sentence which we could wish otherwise written; nor are the surrounding group of correspondents unworthy of the central figure. In this respect their various theoretical opinions seem to make little difference; but we soon feel that it is not from a chosen company ol men such as these that we can argue as to the ultimate influence of any belief or disbelief upon the mass of mankind. Ignorant and prejudiced critics are the only villains in the tale, and even their howling comes to us faint as the wolfish sounds which Æneas heard across the waters as he steered safe by Circe's isle. How different from the restless bitterness of

Carlyle, who makes us feel that he is struggling alone to retain reason and humanity among the crowding bears and swine ! — from the sad resolve of George Eliot, who seems ever to be encountering the enchantress with the sprig of moly—herself half doubtful of its power !

And linked with this peace of conscience there is a boyish yet a steadfast happiness ; a total freedom from our self-questioning complexities—from the *Welt-Schmerz* which, in one form or other, has paralysed or saddened so many of the best lives of our time.   Can we get nearer to the sources of this tranquillity ? Can we detect the prophylactic which kept the melancholy infection at bay ?

It is again in Darwin's own lucid analysis of his intellectual life (i. 100) that we find the answer to our question.

I have said that in one respect my mind has changed during the last twenty or thirty years.   Up to the age of thirty, or beyond it, poetry of many kinds, such as the works of Milton, Gray, Byron, Wordsworth, Coleridge, and Shelley, gave me great pleasure, and even as a schoolboy I took great delight in Shakespeare, especially in the historical plays.   I have also said that formerly pictures gave me considerable, and music very great delight.   But now for many years I cannot endure to read a line of poetry; I have tried lately to read Shakespeare, and found it so intolerably dull that it nauseated me. I have also almost lost my taste for pictures or music. Music generally sets me thinking too energetically on what I have been at work on, instead of giving me pleasure. My mind seems to have become a kind of machine for grinding general laws out of large collections of facts, but why this should have caused the atrophy of that part of the brain alone on which the higher tastes depend, I cannot conceive. . . . The loss of these tastes is a loss of happiness, and may possibly be injurious to the intellect, and more probably to the moral character, by enfeebling the emotional part of our nature.

Here, surely, is the solution of the problem. The faculties of observation and reasoning were stimulated to the utmost; the domestic affections were kept keen and strong; but the atrophy of the religious instincts, of which we have already spoken, extended yet further— over the whole range of aesthetic emotion, of mystic sentiment—over all in us which "looks before and after, and pines for what is not." And although Darwin himself suggests that his intellectual or moral nature may thus have been injured, we may perhaps, on the agnostic hypothesis, more truly say that his intellect was thus fruitfully constrained and his moral nature

saved from shock and storm ; nay, we may go
on to argue that for all of us such limitation
would be best, and that the poets should be
crowned with flowers and led out for ever from
the agnostic city ; and that art altogether—not
only its lower forms, tinged with a human
passion, but its higher forms, tinged with a
divine — must needs produce on the whole
more of pain than of pleasure, more of yearning than of fruition, in a race whose aspirations
are for ever withering " at the touch of Eld
and Death."

In Darwin these vague emotions could have
found no root of baser passion round which to
twine. Yet even for him there must have been
moments which, if too thrillingly repeated,
would have jeopardised his inward peace ; as
when sitting (i. 49), like Milton, in the dim
religious light that falls from the storied
windows of King's College Chapel he heard the
organ pealing of those ineffable things which,
if they may not make man's happiness, must
make man's woe.

And while the limitations of his nature in
one direction secured his tranquillity, its extraordinary vigour in another direction—his

strength of scientific curiosity, his passion for the discovery of new truth——gave the impulse which carried him cheerfully across bodily sufferings so prolonged and weary that for most men they would have darkened the whole track of life.   Now, looking at Darwin's nature as offering us the best agnostic pattern, we see at once that, even assuming that we can imitate its restrictions, we cannot imitate its activity. We cannot hope to rival his inventiveness, his scientific power.   If we, too, are to live contented with scientific progress, this means that most of us must find our happiness in the mere contemplation of the work of others——that the exhilarating sense of men's ever-widening outlook must compensate the paltriness of our individual lots.

This is a great reduction, but this is not yet all.   For even here a doubt steals in, a doubt at which one smiles at first, as Mill learnt to smile at his (quite reasonable) fear that musical combinations would in time be exhausted, but which recurs irresistibly so soon as we try to give distinctness to the popular or optimist view of the future of science.   It is taken for granted in popular writings that the present

rush of scientific progress is to go on indefinitely ; that in proportion as the skill and
energy devoted to research increase, the discoveries made will be ever more numerous and
exciting.   But in truth if (as is commonly
assumed) our discoveries are confined to the
physical side of things, there is no ground
whatever for this sanguine hope.   Admitting
that the visible universe is, in relation to our
present faculties, practically infinite, it by no
means follows that our means of scrutinising it
are capable of indefinite improvement.   And in
fact we find the true pioneers of science greatly
more cautious in their prognostic.   We begin
to hear that telescopy and microscopy (which
in their brief existence have suggested so many
more problems than they have solved) are
already approaching ominously near to their
theoretic limit.   We begin to recognise in the
length of the light-wave an irreducible bar to
that scrutiny of the " infinitely little " which we
most urgently need.   We begin to feel that
the sensitiveness of the retina, the percipient
power of the brain, however supplemented by
sensitive apparatus, must always be inadequate
to the more delicate tasks which we would fain

assign to them ; and in short that the human
body, developed for quite other purposes, must
always be a rude and clumsy instrument for
the apprehension of abstract truth.   And more
than this.   Vast as is the visible universe,
infinite as may have been the intelligence
which went to its evolution, yet while viewed
in the external way in which alone we can view
it, — while seen as a product and not as a
plan, — it cannot possibly suggest to us an
indefinite number of universal laws.   Such
cosmic generalisations as gravitation, evolution,
correlation of forces, conservation of energy,
though assuredly as yet unexhausted, cannot
in the nature of things be even approximately
inexhaustible.

Man's history, in short, is as yet in its first
chapter, and science has lived as yet but a
moment in the brief history of man ; yet
already, and, so to say, with the first glance
out of our prison-windows, we have seen
enough to make it tolerably certain that after
a few more centuries the number of first-rate
discoveries must constantly lessen, while the
number of men equipped and eager for discovery will constantly increase.   Unless, indeed,

some insight is gained into the psychical side
of things, some communication realised with
intelligences outside our own, some light thrown
upon a more than corporeal descent and destiny
of man,[1] it would seem that the shells to be
picked up on the shore of the ocean of truth
will become ever scantier, and the agnostics of
the future will gaze forth ever more hopelessly
on that gloomy and unvoyageable sea.

Such men will look back to Darwin as half-
hearted Christians of to-day look back to those
who expected themselves to witness the glorious consummation of all. "In this man's life,"
they will say, "we see the happy moment, the
best that fate could do for humankind. She
wrought him without a flaw ; she left in him
not one secret sting of restless egotism, of unlawful desire. She gave intellectual vigour,
innocent affections, the dignity of pains bravely
borne. To all this we too might aspire. But
she gave him also the one thing needful ; the
joy in which we can never share. For she

---

[1] "This is an experiment after my own heart," says Darwin
(ii. 57) of one of his trials to make an unlikely seed germinate,
"with chances 1000 to 1 against its success." The human race
will have to try many experiments not less unpromising, if they
do not choose to resign themselves to looking at the world from
without, instead of from within.

inspired him with a majestic conception ; she set him on the track of truths so great and new that they seemed to fill the whole horizon, and transfigured life with their glow. Our knowledge is a hundredfold greater than his. But its ardour, its illusions are no more. For we know at last that nothing which we shall ever discover can be to us of any true concern. What profit, if we are to gaze upon the Cosmos for ever from outside? to pass and leave the giant forces playing, with a purport (if any purport) which is for ever hid from men? What gain, to watch for an hour the inscrutable pageant? to be summoned out of nothingness into illusion, and evolved but to aspire and to decay!"

THE DISENCHANTMENT
OF FRANCE
(1888)

Quod procul a nobis flectat Fortuna gubernans !
Et ratio potius quam res persuadeat ipsa
Succidere horrisono posse omnia victa fragore.

LUCRETIUS.

IT has fallen to the lot of the French people
to point more morals, to emphasise more
lessons from their own experience than any
other nation in modern history. Parties and
creeds of the most conflicting types have
appealed to Paris in turn for their brightest
example, their most significant warning. The
strength of monarchy and the risks of des-
potism ; the nobility of faith, and the cruel
cowardice of bigotry ; the ardour of republican
fraternity and the terrors of anarchic disin-
tegration—the most famous instance of any
and every extreme is to be found in the long

annals of France.   And so long as the French
mind, at once logical and mobile, continues to
be the first to catch and focus the influences
which are slowly beginning to tell on neigh-
bouring States, so long will its evolution possess
for us the unique interest of a glimpse into
stages of development through which our own
national mind also may be destined ere long
to pass.

Yet there has of late been a kind of re-
luctance on the part of other civilised countries
to take to themselves the lessons which French
history still can teach.   In Germany there has
been a tone of reprobation, an opposition of
French vice to Teuton virtue ; and in England
there has been some aloofness of feeling, some
disposition to think that the French have
fallen through their own fault into a decadence
which our robuster nation need not fear.

In the brief review, however, which this
essay will contain of certain gloomy symptoms
in the spiritual state of France we shall keep
entirely clear of any disparaging comparisons
or insinuated blame.   Rather we shall regard
France as the most sensitive organ of the
European body politic ; we shall feel that her

dangers of to-day are ours of to-morrow, and
that unless there still be salvation for her our
own prospects are dark indeed.

But in the first place, it may be asked,
what right have we to speak of France as
decadent at all ?   The word, indeed, is so constantly employed by French authors of the
day that the foreigner may assume without
impertinence that there is some fitness in its
use.   Yet have we here much more than a
fashion of speaking ? the humour of men who
are " sad as night for very wantonness," who
play with the notion of national decline as a
rich man in temporary embarrassment may
play with the notion of ruin ?   France is
richer and more populous than ever before ;
her soldiers still fight bravely, and the mass
of her population, as judged by the statistics
of crime, or by the colourless half-sheet which
forms the only national newspaper,[1] is at any
rate tranquil and orderly.   Compare the state

[1] *Le Petit Journal* has a circulation of nearly a million.
What it does contain, or why it is taken, it might be hard to
say ; but at least it does *not* contain anything which could raise
a blush, or prompt to an unlawful action.   Provincial life in
France seldom finds literary expression (see Theuriet, Pierre
Loti, Ferdinand Fabre) ; when it rises to a certain intellectual
level it seems to merge irresistibly into the life of Paris.

of France now with her state just a century
since, before the outbreak of the Revolution. Observers who noted that misgovernment
and misery, those hordes of bandits prowling
over the untilled fields, assumed it as manifest
that not the French monarchy only but France
herself was crumbling in irremediable decay.
And yet a few years later the very children
reared as half slaves, half beggars, on black-bread
and ditch-water were marching with banners
flying into Vienna and Moscow. One must be
wary in predicting the decline of a nation which
holds in reserve a spring of energy such as this.

Once more. Not physically alone but
intellectually France has never, perhaps, been
stronger than she is now. She is lacking, indeed, in statesmen of the first order, in poets
and artists of lofty achievement, and, if our
diagnosis be correct, she must inevitably lack
such men as these. But on the other hand
her living *savants* probably form as wise, as
disinterested a group of intellectual leaders as
any epoch of her history has known. And
she listens to them with a new deference ; she
receives respectfully even the bitter home-
truths of M. Taine ; she honours M. Renan

instead of persecuting him ; she makes M.
Pasteur her national hero. These men and
men like these are virtually at the head of
France ; and if the love of truth, the search
for truth, fortifies a nation, then assuredly
France should be stronger now than under any
of her kings or her Caesars.

Yet here we come to the very crux of the
whole inquiry. If we maintain that an increasing knowledge of truth is necessarily a
strength or advantage to a nation or an
individual, we are assuming an affirmative
answer to two weighty questions : the first,
whether, the scheme of the universe is on the
whole good rather than evil ; the second,
whether, even granting that the sum of things
is good, each advancing step of our knowledge
of the universe brings with it an increased
realisation of that ultimate goodness. Of
course if we return to the first question the
pessimistic answer—if the world is a bad place
and cosmic suicide the only reasonable thing
—the present discussion may at once be closed.
For in that case there is no such thing as
progress, no such thing as recovery ; and the
moral discouragement of France does but

indicate her advance upon the road which we must all inevitably travel.

Let us assume, however, as is commonly assumed without too curious question, that the universe is good, and that to know the truth about it is on the whole an invigorating thing. Yet even thus it is by no means clear that each onward step we make in learning that truth will in itself be felt as invigorating. All analogy is against such a supposition ; whether we turn to the history of philosophy, and the depression repeatedly following on the collapse of specious but premature conceptions, or to the history of individual minds, and the despair of the beginner in every art or study when he recognises that he has made a false start ; that he knows almost nothing ; that the problems are far more difficult than his ignorance had suspected.

Now I think it is not hard to show that France, even on the most hopeful view of her, is at present passing through a moment of spiritual reaction such as this. In that country where the pure dicta of science reign in the intellectual classes with less interference from custom, sentiment, tradition than even in

Germany itself, we shall find that science, at her present point, is a depressing, a disintegrating energy.

And therefore when we compare the present state of France with her state a century ago, we must not rank her dominant *savants* as a source of national strength. Rather they are a source of disenchantment, of *disillusionment*, to use the phrase of commonest recurrence in modern French literature and speech. Personally, indeed, the class of *savants* includes many an example of unselfish diligence, of stoical candour, but their virtues are personal to themselves, and the upshot of their teaching affords no stable basis for virtue.

We may say, then, that in 1888 France possesses everything except illusions ; in 1788 she possessed illusions and nothing else. The Reign of Reason, the Return to Nature, the Social Contract, Liberty, Equality, Fraternity —the whole air of that wild time buzzed with new-hatched Chimæras, while at the same time the old traditions of Catholicism, Loyalty, Honour, were still living in many an ardent heart.

What, then, is in effect the disenchantment

which France has undergone ?   What are the
illusions—the so-called, so-judged illusions—
which are fading now before the influence of
science ?   How is a foreigner to analyse the
confused changes in a great people's spiritual
life ?   Must not his own personal acquaintance
with Frenchmen, which is sure to be slight and
shallow, unduly influence his judgment of the
nation ?   It seems to me that he must set
aside his personal acquaintanceships and form
his opinion from current literature and current
events ; endeavouring so far as may be to
elicit such general views of life as may be latent
in the varying utterances of novelist, essayist,
politician, philosopher, and poet.   Thus reading
and thus comparing, we shall discern a gradual
atrophy of certain habits of thought, certain
traditional notions ; and if we class as *illusions*
these old conceptions from which the French
people seems gradually to be awakening, we find
them reducible to four main heads ; the *religious*,
the *political*, the *sexual*, and the *personal* illusions.

I. By the " religious illusion "—speaking, it
will be remembered, from the point of view of
the Frenchman of the type now under discussion
—I mean a belief in the moral government of

the world, generally involving a belief in man's future life, in which life we may suppose virtue victorious and earth's injustices redressed. These cardinal beliefs, now everywhere on the defensive, are plainly losing ground in France more rapidly than elsewhere. And the strange thing is that while Christianity thus declines it seems to leave in France so little regret behind it ; that its disappearance is signalised only by loud battles between "Liberalism" and "Clericalism," not, as in England, by sad attempts at reconciliation, by the regrets and appeals of slowly - severing men. A book like Chateaubriand's *Génie du Christianisme*, nay even a book like Lamennais' *Paroles d'un Croyant*, would now be felt to be an anachronism. Militant Catholicism seems almost to have died out with M. Veuillot's articles in the *Univers;* and an application to a high ecclesiastical authority for recent defences of the faith brought to me only a recommendation to read the Bishops' Charges, the *mandements d'évêque*. Paradox as it may seem, M. Renan is almost the only French writer of influence who believes that Christianity — of course a Christianity without miracles—will be in any sense the

religion of the future ; and his recent utterances
show that pious sentiment, in his hands, is
liable to sudden and unexpected transformations.
A passage from the preface to his play *L'Abbesse
de Jouarre* (1886) will illustrate the facility with
which " the cult of the ideal " when freed from
" the support of superstition " flows along lines
of least resistance, and into a less austere and
strenuous mould.

The Abbess, too intelligent to believe in the
dogmas which (from the highest motives) she
has outwardly supported, and finding herself,
under the Reign of Terror, confronted with the
immediate prospect of death, yields (from the
highest motives) to the solicitations of a fellow-
prisoner, who ardently admires her. But it so
happens that she is *not* guillotined ; and she
afterwards experiences a delicate distress in
reconciling what may be termed the morality
of great crises to the conventions of ordinary
life. In a passage which in these pages I can
only partially quote M. Renan explains and
defends her.

That which, at the hour of death, must needs
assume a character of absolute sincerity, is love.   I
often imagine that if humanity were to acquire the

certain knowledge that the world was to come to an
end in two or three days, love would break out on
every side with a sort of frenzy ; for love is held in
check only by the absolutely necessary restrictions
which the moral preservation of human society has
imposed.   When one perceived oneself confronted
by a sudden and certain death, nature alone would
speak ; the strongest of her instincts, constantly
checked and thwarted, would reassume its rights ; a
cry would burst from every breast when one knew
that one might approach with perfect lawfulness the
tree guarded by so many anathemas. . . . The world's
last sigh would be as it were a kiss of sympathy
addressed to the universe—and perhaps to somewhat
that is beyond.   One would die in the sentiment of
the highest adoration, and in the most perfect act of
prayer. . . .

I hope that my Abbess may please those idealists
who have no need to believe in the existence of dis-
embodied spirits in order to believe in duty, and who
know that moral nobility does not depend on metaphysical opinions.   In these days one hears men for
ever talking—and from the most opposite camps—of
the enfeeblement of religious beliefs.   How careful,
in such a matter, one should be to avoid misunder-
standing !   Religious beliefs transform themselves ;
they lose their symbolical envelope, which is a mere
encumbrance, and have no further need of the support
of superstition.   But the philosopher's soul is unaffected by these necessary evolutions.   The true,
the beautiful, the good are in themselves sufficiently
attractive to need no authority which shall ordain, nor
reward which shall sanction them.   Love, especially,
will for ever maintain its sacred character.   Modern

paradoxes inspire me with no more anxiety as to the persistence of the cult of the ideal than as to the perpetuation of the race. The danger would begin only on that day when women ceased to be fair, flowers to open voluptuously, birds to sing. In our temperate climes, and among our pleasure-loving peoples, this danger, thank God, seems still sufficiently remote.

The ancient maxim, " Let us eat and drink, for to-morrow we die," has never lacked, and will never lack, its eager advocates ; but this is perhaps the first time that it has been preached as virtually *identical* with that very religion to which " le fougueux apôtre," as M. Renan gently terms St. Paul, imagined it to be directly *opposed.* The best *pendant* to the optimistic hymn above quoted may be found in a passage from M. Bourget, a critic of no starched austerity nor bigoted temper, but whose imagination pictures the mind of our successors when the flowers, the birds, the women, delight no more ; when the thorns, to speak with Biblical plainness, have ceased to crackle under the pot.

Science (he says) has rendered it impossible to repose faith in any supernatural revelation, while at the same time she proclaims herself unable to unriddle the problems of which revelation offered a solution. There are some who have thought to find the remedy for this new and singular crisis by imagining the human race in the future as delivered from all thought of the Beyond, and indifferent to what we call the Absolute.   But this is a gratuitous hypothesis, and seems little in harmony with the general march of thought.   We have a better right, on the other hand, to predict that civilisation as it advances will subtilise ever further our nervous sensibility—will develop the weary sadness of hearts which no known pleasure satisfies, and whose unquenchable ardour yearns to slake itself at some inexhaustible spring.   It is probable that in the final bankruptcy of hope to which science is leading us, many of these souls will sink into a despair such as Pascal would have sunk into had he lost his faith.   The gulf whence we issue painfully, and which with pain we re-enter, will open itself before them, for ever black and void.   There will be revolts of spirit, rebellions more typical than any age has known.   Life will be unbearable with the knowledge that there is no more hope of under-standing it, and that the same sign of fruitless ques-tion hangs for ever over the horizon of man.   It will not be strange if in those days a sect of nihilists should arise, possessed with a frenzy of destruction such as those alone can comprehend who have felt within themselves the tightening clutch of spiritual death.   To know that one cannot know—to be assured that no assurance is possible—ah, cruel anguish! which, spreading like a plague through the millions of men, will summon them as it were to an anti-crusade—a war against the spirit.   Then in that day, and if the nightmare which I am evoking becomes fact indeed, other souls, gentler and more inclined to a happy interpretation of man's fate, will

oppose to this rebellious pessimism an optimism of
melancholy peace.   If the problem of the universe is
insoluble, an answer may be conjectured which harmonises with our moral needs, our emotional cravings.
The hypothesis of hope has its chance of being true
no less than the hypothesis of despair.   In M. Renan
we have a finished exemplar of the religious senti-
ments which would unite the uncertain believers of
that cruel age ; and who shall venture to assert that
the impulse of formless faith which sums up the disenchanted optimism of this historian of our dying
religion does not express the essence of all of worship
that shall remain immortal in this splendid and miserable temple which is the heart of man ?

II. Let us pass on to the second class of
illusions from which France seems finally to
have awakened.   Under the title of " the political illusion " we may include two divergent yet
not wholly disparate emotions—the enthusiasm
of loyalty and the enthusiasm of equality.
Each of these enthusiasms has done in old
times great things for France ; each in turn has
seemed to offer a self-evident, nay a divine
organisation of the perplexed affairs of men.
But each in turn has lost its efficacy.   There
is now scarcely a name but General Boulanger's
in France which will raise a cheer ; scarcely
even a Socialistic Utopia for which a man
would care to die.   The younger nations,

accustomed to look to France for inspiration, feel the dryness of that ancient source. " Ils ne croient à rien," said a Russian of the Nihilists, " mais ils ont besoin du martyre." The Nihilists, indeed, are like the lemmings, which swim out to sea in obedience to an instinct that bids them seek a continent long since sunk beneath the waves. Gentle anarchists, pious atheists, they follow the blind instinct of self-devotion which makes the force of a naïve, an unworldly people. But there is now no intelligible object of devotion left for them to seek ; and they go to the mines and to the gibbet without grasping a single principle or formulating a single hope. These are the pupils of modern France ; but in France herself the nihilistic disillusionment works itself out unhindered by the old impulse to die for an idea. The French have died for too many ideas already ; and just as they have ceased to idealise man's relationship to God, so have they ceased at last to idealise his relationship to his fellow-men.

III. But the process of disillusionment can be traced deeper still. Closer to us, in one sense, than our relation to the universe as a whole, more intimate than our relation to our fellow-citizens, is the mutual relation between the sexes. An emotion such as love, at once vague, complex, and absorbing, is eminently open to fresh interpretation as the result of modern analysis. And on comparing what may be called the enchanted and disenchanted estimates of this passion—the view of Plato, for instance, and the view of Schopenhauer— we find that the discordance goes to the very root of the conception ; that what in Plato's view is the accident is in Schopenhauer's the essential ; that what Plato esteemed as the very aim and essence is for Schopenhauer a delusive figment, a witchery cast over man's young inexperience, from which adult reason should shake itself wholly free. For Plato the act of idealisation which constitutes love is closely akin to the act of idealisation which constitutes worship. The sudden passion which carries the lover beyond all thought of self is the result of a memory and a yearning which the beloved one's presence stirs within him—a memory of antenatal visions, a yearning towards the home of the soul. The true end of love is mutual ennoblement ; its fruition lies in the unseen. Or if we look to its earthly issue,

it is not children only who are born from such
unions as these, but from that fusion of earnest
spirits great thoughts, just laws, noble institutions
spring, " a fairer progeny than any child of man."

Not one of the speculations of antiquity
outdid in lofty originality this theme of Plato's.
And, however deeply the changing conditions
of civilisation might modify the outward forms
or setting of love, this far-reaching conception
has been immanent in the poet's mind, and
has made of love an integral element in the
spiritual scheme of things.   " Love was given,"
says Wordsworth in a poem which strangely
harmonises the antique and the modern ideal——

> Love was given,
> Encouraged, sanctioned, chiefly for that end ;
> For this the passion to excess was driven—
> That self might be annulled ; her bondage prove
> The fetters of a dream, opposed to Love.

And even when the passion has not been thus
directly linked with ethical aims it has been
credited with a heaven-sent, a mysterious
charm ; like the beauty and scent of flowers,
it has been regarded as a joy given to us for
the mere end of joy.

In recent years, however, a wholly different

aspect of the passion of love has been raised into prominence. This new theory—for it is hardly less—is something much deeper than the mere satirical depreciation, the mere ascetic horror, of the female sex. It recognises the mystery, the illusion, the potency of love, but it urges that this dominating illusion is no heaven-descended charm of life, but the result of terrene evolution, and that, so far from being salutary to the individual, it is expressly designed to entrap him into subserving the ends of the *race*, even when death to himself (or herself) is the immediate consequence. It was in England that the facts in natural history which point to this conclusion were first set forth ; it was in Germany that a philosophical theory was founded (even before most of those facts were known) upon these blind efforts of the race, working through the passions of the individual, yet often to his ruin ; but it is in France that we witness the actual entry of this theory into the affairs of life—the gradual dissipation of the " sexual illusion " which nature has so long been weaving with unconscious magic around the senses and the imagination of man.

In the first place, then, human attractiveness has suffered something of the same loss of
romance which has fallen upon the scent and
colour of flowers, since we have realised that
these have been developed as an attraction to
moths and other insects, whose visits to the
flower are necessary to secure effective fertilisa-
tion.   Our own attractiveness in each other's
eyes seems no longer to point to some divine
reminiscence ; rather it is a character which
natural and sexual selection must needs have
developed if our race was to persist at all ;
and it is paralleled by elaborate and often
grotesque æsthetic allurements throughout the
range of organised creatures of separate sex.

Once more.   The great Roman poet of
" wheat and woodland, tilth and vineyard, hive
and horse and herd," insisted long ago on
the divergence, throughout animated nature, of
the promptings of amorous passion and of
self-preservation.   Passing beyond the facile
optimism of pastoral singers, he showed the
peace, the strength, the life of the animal
creation at the mercy of an instinct which
they can neither comprehend nor disobey.   *In
furias ignemque ruunt.*   Advancing science

has both confirmed and explained this profound observation.   She has discovered instances where the instinct in question conducts
not merely to a remote and contingent but to
an immediate and inevitable death, and where
yet it works itself out with unfailing punctuality.
And she has demonstrated that in the race of
races the individual must not pause for breath ;
his happiness, his length of days, must be
subordinated to the supreme purpose of leaving
a progeny which can successfully prolong the
endless struggle.   And here the bitter philosophy of Schopenhauer steps in, and shows that
as man rises from the savage state the form of
the illusive witchery changes, but the witchery
is still the same.   Nature is still prompting us
to subserve the advantage of the race—an
advantage which is not our own—though she
uses now such delicate baits as artistic admiration, spiritual sympathy, the union of kindred
souls.   Behind and beneath all these is still
her old unconscious striving ; but she can
scarcely any longer outwit us ; we now desire
neither the pangs of passion, nor the restraints
of marriage, nor the burden of offspring ; while
for the race we need care nothing, or may even

deem it best and most merciful that the race itself should lapse and pass away.

The insensible advance of this sexual disenchantment will show itself first and most obviously in the imaginative literature of a nation. And the transition from Romanticism to so-called Naturalism in fiction which is the conspicuous fact of the day in France is ill understood if it be taken to be a mere change in literary fashion, a mere reaction against sentimental and stylistic extravagance. The Naturalists claim, and the claim is just, that they seek at least a closer analogy with the methods of Science herself; that they rest, not on fantastic fancies, but on the *documents humains* which are furnished by the actual life of every day. But, on the other hand, the very fact that this is all which they desire to do is enough to prove that even this will scarcely be worth the doing. The fact that they thus shrink from idealising bespeaks an epoch barren in ideal. Schopenhauer boasted that he had destroyed " die Dame," the chivalrous conception of woman as a superior being ; and such novels as those of Flaubert, Zola, Maupassant Huysmans, exhibit the world with

this illusion gone.   If, moreover, the relations
between men and women are not kept, in a
sense, *above* the relations between men and
men, they will rapidly fall *below* them.   We
are led into a world of joyless vice from the
sheer decay of the conception of virtue.

Mr. Henry James's analysis of M. de Maupassant's works will be fresh in many recollections.   And I may add some corroborative
words, not from Scherer or Brunetière or any
critic who stands upon the ancient ways, and
whose disapproval may be discounted beforehand, but from the friendly pen of M. Lemaître,
whose description is not meant to carry moral
reprobation along with it.

M. de Maupassant, too, is affected with that
newest malady of authors—namely, pessimism, and
the strange desire to represent the world as ugly and
brutal, governed by blind instincts . . . and at the
same time to exhibit with an amount of detail never
previously equalled this world, which is neither interesting in itself nor as a subject of art ; so that the
pleasure which the writer and the reader who com-
prehends him enjoy is derived only from irony,
pride, egoistic gratification.   There is here no thought
of what was once termed the ideal, no preoccupation
with morality, no sympathy with mankind, but at
most a contemptuous pity of the absurd and wretched
race of men.   On the other hand, we find a scientific

H

skill in playing with the world as an object of sense,
apt for our delectation; the interest which is refused
to things in themselves is bestowed wholly on the
art of rendering them in a form as plastic as possible.
On the whole, the attitude is that of some misan-
thropic, scornful, and lascivious god.[1]

Yet neither this criticism nor Mr. Henry
James's exhibits fully, as it seems to me, the
essential weakness and emptiness of M. de
Maupassant and others of the same school.
Their vigour is the mere expression of their
own youth and health, cleverness and prosperity; there is no indication of any reserve
of moral strength, of any stoical courage, any
assured philosophy which would render them
in a true sense superiors of the objects of their
contemptuous dissection. A few lines from
M. Bourget, describing the disciples of Flaubert,
will illustrate my meaning here.

They exhibit the human animal as dominated by
his environment, and almost incapable of an individual reaction against surrounding things. Hence
springs that despairing fatalism which is the philosophy of all the existing school of novelists. Hence
the renunciation, ever more marked, of larger hopes,
of generous ardours, of whatsoever among our intimate energies can be called faith in an ideal. And

[1] *Les Contemporains*, p. 301.

since our age is smitten with a malady of the will, the psychology of our fashionable literature adjusts itself to the gradual weakening of the inward spring. Slowly, in many a mind which the romances of our day have shaped, the conviction is formed that effort is useless, that the force of external causes cannot be withstood.[1]

IV. And thus we are brought, by a natural transition, to the fourth and last illusion from which French thought is shaking itself free— the illusion which pervades man more profoundly than any other—the dream of his own free-will, and of his psychical unity. It is in the analysis of this *personal illusion* that much of the acutest French work has lately been done ; it is here that ordinary French opinion is perhaps furthest removed from the English type ; and it is here, moreover, as I shall presently indicate,—it is on this field of experimental psychology, that the decisive battles of the next century seem likely to be fought. In this essay, however, I must keep clear of detail, and must touch only on the general effect of the mass of teaching of which Taine and Ribot on the psychological side, Charcot and Richet on the physiological side, may serve as repre-

[1] *Essais de psychologie contemporaine,* 1st series, p. 166.

sentatives. These names might be supplemented by many more ; and indeed it is in
this direction of physiological psychology, in
the widest sense, that the strongest stream of
French intellect seems to me to be at present
flowing.

As regards the freedom of the will, indeed,
it might have been supposed that the controversy had now been waged too long to admit
of much accession of novel argument. Nor,
of course, can any theory which we hold as
to human free-will reasonably influence our
actions one way or the other. Yet we know
that as a matter of actual observation Mahom-
medan fatalism does influence conduct, and
the determinism which is becoming definitely
the creed of France may similarly be traced
throughout their modern pictures of life and
character as a paralysing influence in moments
of decisive choice, of moral crisis. The following passage from a writer of recognised
authority will show the unhesitating way in
which the French mind presses home conclusions which, though based in a large measure
on English doctrines, are seldom so trenchantly
formulated at home :—

Is personality (inquires M. Ribot), is character independent of heredity ? The problem is important, since it involves the question whether the power of heredity has any assignable limit. It is plain that there are only two possible hypotheses : we may either admit that at each birth a special act of creation infuses into each being the germ of character and personality, or we may admit that this germ is the product of earlier generations, and is inevitably deduced from the character of the parents and the circumstances under which the new life is originated. The first of these hypotheses is so far from scientific that it is not worth discussing. We are left to the second view. And here we find ourselves brought abruptly back to the very heart of our subject. We thought that we were escaping from heredity, and now we find it in that very germ which forms the most intimate and personal element of our being. After having shown by a long enumeration of facts that the sensitive and intellectual faculties are transmitted, that one may inherit a given instinct, a given passion, a given type of imagination, just as easily as a tendency to consumption, to rickets, to longevity, we hoped at least that a part of the psychic life lay outside determinism, that the character, the person, the self, escaped the law of heredity; but no, heredity, which is equivalent to determinism, envelops us on every side, without and within.[1]

We have now traced the spread in France of what I have termed disenchantment over the main departments of moral and intellectual

[1] *L'hérédité psychologique*, 2nd edit. p. 323.

life. It might remain to ask whether any
definite test exists, reducible to numbers, by
which we can measure the effect on national
prosperity of this less firm and eager grasp on
existence.   This might be attempted in many
ways, although, considering the subtlety of the
motives at work, we cannot expect more than
an inferential, an approximate result.   Setting
aside in this essay the subject of relative
frequency of *suicide* (where the comparison
between one nation and another is much com-
plicated by differences in the material welfare
of the lower classes), I will briefly consider in
what way this disenchanted temper affects the
central problem of the French publicist—the
practical cessation of the growth of population.
" A vrai dire, c'est le péril national tout entier,"
says Professor Richet of this check in numbers ;
" il n'en existe pas d'autre."

To us in England, of course, the opposite
view is more familiar.   We feel the perils not
of defect of population but of excess ; and so
far as our own comfort is concerned we should
be glad indeed if our numbers were as stationary
as in France.   And if all European nations
agreed to limit population—just as if all nations

agreed to disarm—an epoch of marked material prosperity would no doubt ensue. At present, however, there seems no chance whatever of this, and we are engaged in a general scramble to overstock our own countries, and thence to overspread the earth. A nation which falls out of this scramble may gain in comfort for the time, but it will lose its status ; its specific type will become relatively unimportant ; its thought and literature will lose their power with mankind. Great and powerful though France is now, such countries as Holland and Belgium are not without their warning for her in the near future. In fifty years, if the present rates of increase are maintained, she will rank sixth only among European nations. In 150 years she will have sunk almost beneath consideration in a world of Russians and Germans, Anglo-Saxons and Chinese.[1]   Without repro-

---

[1] See Professor Charles Richet's articles in the *Revue des Deux Mondes*, April 15 and June 1, 1882 ; and M. E. Cheysson's paper in *La réforme sociale*, July 1, 1883. M. Guyau in his *L'irréligion de l'aveuir* (p. 274, etc.) draws out the connection between this decline in population and the decay of religious belief. As between Brittany and Normandy, for instance, the difference is not due to Norman prudence alone ; for the Breton is also prudent, but in a different way ;—he postpones marriage till (at an average age of thirty-four for men, twenty-nine for women) a property sufficient for a good-sized family has been amassed.

ducing the elaborate computations by which
the relative decline of France has been ex-
hibited by statisticians, it is enough to say that
in the present acute phase of national com-
petition France cannot afford to forego the
motive power of the *ver sacrum*—of yearly
swarms of young men pressing forward to
develop their country either by colonisation
without her borders, or by novel and eager
enterprise within. At the same time it is of
course desirable that multiplication should be
combined with *providence*—that the increase of
numbers should not proceed from the lowest
and most reckless classes alone. Now in comparing the natality or rate of increase of
different provinces in France, it seems that the
increase is rapid in two main quarters—first (as
with ourselves) among the degraded inhabitants
of the poorer quarters of great cities, and
secondly in those provinces where Catholicism
is still a dominant power. Between Catholic
Brittany and free-thinking Normandy the contrast is striking ; and the more so inasmuch as
the difference of *race* between these provinces
seems all in favour of the Norman population,
whose young mothers, indeed, are in special

request for the benefit of infants other than
their own.   Yet the annual births in Brittany
are thirty-three for each thousand of population ; in Normandy only nineteen.

Now in the educated classes, where rapidity
of increase is still more important, the impulses
in either direction, though less crudely defined,
are not therefore less potent.   On the one side
there is the wish for new objects of affection
and the satisfaction with the lot upon which
the children will enter ; on the other side,
besides the obvious economical reasons,
there is the decline in the value set upon
existence and the doubt whether it is well to
summon new beings as sensitive as ourselves
into a world which to each fresh generation
seems to loom more awful in the obscurity of
its meaning and of its end.

A few quotations may show that this is no
imaginary picture ; and my first instance shall
be taken from the loftiest, the sincerest of living
French poets—the author whose name comes
first to the lips of a Frenchman, challenged to
prove that the tradition of " high thinking " is
not yet extinct.   In his poem *Le vœu* M.
Sully-Prudhomme draws the following practical

lesson from a contemplation of the misery of
man :—

Du plus aveugle instinct je me veux rendre maître,
Hélas ! non par vertu, mais par compassion.
Dans l'invisible essaim des condamnés à naître,
Je fais grâce à celui dont je sens l'aiguillon.

Demeure dans l'empire innommé du possible,
O fils le plus aimé qui ne naîtras jamais !
Mieux sauvé que les morts et plus inaccessible,
Tu ne sortiras pas de l'ombre où je dormais !

These words do not fall from a mere fantastic
artist ; they come from a philosopher and
moralist, a man of strong human sympathies,
and who by no means despairs altogether of
the future of mankind. I pass on to the
passionate cry of an avowed, but not a morbid,
pessimist. I must not here stop to discuss
Madame Ackermann, one of the most significant
figures in contemporary literature ; but it should
be understood that her sadness is in no way a
personal matter, but represents the impression
irresistibly wrought upon her by the mere
" riddle of the painful earth." I quote the lines
which close her poem on *Pascal* with the wild
conception of some such insult offered to man's
distant and cruel Lord as might move Him to

shiver into fragments this planet which is our scene of pain.

Notre audace du moins vous sauverait de naître,
Vous qui dormez encore au fond de l'avenir,
Et nous triompherions d'avoir, en cessant d'être,
Avec l'Humanité forcé Dieu d'en finir.
Ah ! quelle immense joie après tant de souffrance !
A travers les débris, par-dessus les charniers,
Pouvoir enfin jeter ce cri de délivrance :
Plus d'hommes sous le ciel, nous sommes les derniers!

I will call one more witness ; this time a less serious but still a noteworthy personage ; a novelist who by a certain mixture of Flemish realism and Parisian perversity has become the most advanced (I do not say the ablest) representative both of the decadent and of the naturalistic school.

M. J. K. Huysmans, speaking through the mouth of his decrepit hero, Des Esseintes, strenuously deprecates the cruelty of adding fresh sufferers to the condemned-list of miserable men ; nay, he carries his propagandist (or anti-propagandist) zeal so far as to recommend the legislation of infanticide, and to denounce the child-saving labours of St. Vincent de Paul.

Thanks to his odious precautions, this man had deferred for years the death of creatures without intelligence or sensation, so that becoming later on almost rational, and at any rate capable of pain, they might foresee the future ; might await and dread that Death of which, when he found them, they knew not the very name ; might perhaps even invoke that Death upon themselves, in anger at the condemnation to existence which he inflicted on them in obedience to a ridiculous code of theology.

We have here, I think, indications, as clear as in so complex a matter could be reasonably expected, that this " disenchantment of France," this general collapse of hopes and ideals, does enter as a moral factor into the causes which are now arresting the advance of French population.   If, therefore, population is to receive a fresh impulse, it would seem desirable either that some fresh value should be found for life, or that the race should accustom itself more thoroughly to the narrowed ideal.   And this view is supported, so to say, from the opposite quarter by the growing influence throughout French politics, business, society, of a race whose distinguishing peculiarity lies in the fact that they have already traversed their great disappointment ; that they have learnt at last to silence the heart's infinite appeal ; that they walk among us, but not of us, grimly smiling when our voices repeat, in new tones of yearning, those very phrases from Hebrew psalmist or prophet which the Chosen People themselves have found to fail. For— with the exceptions which sheer atavism must needs produce in the race of a David and a Paul — the modern Jew has crystallised his religion into a mere bond of race ; it steadies rather than disturbs his worldly endeavour, and he stands before us in complete adaptation to changed spiritual conditions, the type of what we all may some day become, if our inward Jerusalem also is destroyed, and the Holy City of our dreams laid level with the dust of the earth. The Jews at one end of the scale, the Chinese at the other—these are the races that have already fitted themselves for a universe without hope. Who shall say that they shall not therefore gradually subdue us ? as after some age-long heaping of sandbanks along a solitary coast the creatures which can first endure the life of land-locked pools will displace those through whose structure runs an indomitable yearning for the tides and vastness of the sea.

The prospect at which we have arrived is a

gloomy one—so gloomy that we instinctively shrink from accepting it as inevitable. There must surely, we feel, be some outlet, some direction in which we may find the dawn of a new hope for France. The classification which we have thus far followed will aid us in an inquiry as to the possible reformation, on a more stable basis, of any of those hopes and beliefs whose evanescence seems to threaten a national decline.

(1) First and most important is the question of religion. And here there are three main channels in which we could imagine a religious revival, in the broadest sense, as tending to flow. We might have a revival in the Christian direction, or in the mystical, or in the Stoic. Any one of these convictions, if sufficiently widespread, might regenerate a nation. But each in turn must be regarded as an *emotional* impulse, as a *subjective* view ; each appeals to minds predisposed to receive it, but fails to convince the egoist or the pessimist by irrefragable logic or indubitable historical proof. As regards Christianity : in the first place, it is scarcely possible that the historical proof can at this late day be materially strengthened.

That proof, we may fairly suppose, will continue to seem adequate to many minds which
nature or grace has cast in the Christian mould.
But as to the Christianity without miracles—the
Theism with a Christian colouring, which in
England is sometimes suggested as a substitute
for the orthodox creeds—for this growth there
seems in France no soil prepared, no temper
from which this religion of compromise could
spring.   The same is the case with mysticism,
and with the *a priori* or affirmative schools of
metaphysic.   Names which command respect
might be cited in either group, but none have
a real hold on the national intelligence.   With
perhaps greater plausibility the neo-Stoics—if
we may so term the agnostics who still cling to
duty and feel their last enthusiasm in resignation to universal law—might claim for their
creed the prospect of ultimate triumph.   Assuredly men like these are essential in every
country, if any high morality is to be upheld
in this ebb of fixed beliefs.   Yet an act of
faith, for which the French mind in general is
ill-prepared, is still necessary if we are to accept
the Cosmos even on Stoic terms.   For there is
a possibility that even here we may be duped

once more ; that we may find *vacuas sedes et
inania templa* in the sanctuary of Duty herself ;
that in the veritable and intimate scheme of
the universe there may be no such conception
as Virtue.

I will not, however, press into my argument
any of the darker currents of French thought
—the cynicism or the pessimism of a Flaubert,
an Ackermann, a Baudelaire. I will rather
sum up the situation in one of the last utterances of a noble mind, "the conclusion of the
whole matter" as it seemed at last to Emile
Littré—once the most enthusiastic of all those
who embraced the too-sanguine synthesis
which still draws back some wistful glances to
the memory of a Worship of Humanity which
has brought little strength to man. The words
which I shall quote are simple and personal ;
but they may stand as the expression of more
than an individual fate.

Voltaire in old age writes in one of his letters
that at the sight of a starry night he was wont to say
to himself that he was about to lose that spectacle ;
that through all eternity he should never see it more.
Like him, I love to contemplate—with the reflection
that it is perhaps for the last time—the starlit night,
the greenness of my garden, the immensity of the

sea.   I go yearly to the seaside ; I went thither this
year.   My room opened upon the beach, and
when the tide was high the waves were but a few
paces from where I sat.   How often did I sink into
contemplation, imagining to myself those Trojan
women who *pontum adspectabant flentes !*   I did not
weep ; but I felt that these solemn spondees best
harmonised with the grandeur of that sight, and with
the vagueness of my own meditations.[1]

Pontum adspectabant flentes !   Fit epigraph
for a race who have fallen from hope, on
whose ears the waves' world-old message still
murmurs without a meaning : while the familiar
landmarks fade backwards into shadow, and
there is nothing but the sea.

(2) As regards the revival of what I have
called the *political illusion,* the enthusiasm
either of loyal subordination or of co-operant
equality, there is no need for much discussion
here.   Changes of some kind impend ; but the
peculiarity of the situation is that from no
change is any real or definite good expected
by reasonable men.   And of course, on the
view taken in this essay, little advantage can
be hoped for a mere *rearrangement* of existing
material—the material in this case being re-

---

[1] *Conservation, Révolution, Positivisme, Remarques,* p. 430.

presented by the beliefs and aspirations of the
best minds of France. There must be, not
rearrangement only, but *renewal*—a fresh in-
flux of hope, conviction, felicity, if outward
institutions are to reflect anything save the
inward uncertainty or despair.

(3) And still more markedly is this the
case as regards that ideal relation between the
sexes which, as I have already intimated,
seems to be in danger of fading in France into
something less permanent and pure. Our
estimate of the value of human affections
must depend largely on our estimate of the
value of human personality itself. Now it is
of course true that the Stoic may rank human
dignity high, though he looks for no individual
survival ; his loves may even take an added
solemnity from the nearness of their final hour.
But from man's transitory state we find French
dramatists and romancers drawing, not *this*, but
the opposite, the more obvious inference ; and
amid all the brevity and instability of human
life there is nothing that seems to him more
brief or more unstable than the passion in
which that life culminates with strongest
charm. There is something melancholy, and

the more melancholy for its very unconscious-
ness, in the way in which *quelques années*
come to be assumed as the natural limit of
any intimate fusion of souls.   A few years!
and the lovers who enter thereupon are resigned already to an ultimate solitude, and
count beforehand the golden moments which
are all that they can steal from fate.

(4) It seems, then, that in our search for
some prospect of a renewal of spiritual energy
in France we are driven back on our fourth
heading, on what I have termed the *personal
illusion ;* or, in other terms, the belief in the
unity and persistence of the personality of
man.   For in no other direction can we foresee
any great change to be effected either by subjective emotion or by scientific discovery.
Speculations on the moral government of the
universe lie too far beyond the range of proof ;
and on the other hand the problems of social
progress and the elevation of the sexual tie
depend in the last resort on what is held to be
the profounder truth as to man's inward being,
and his place in the scheme of things.

But have we any instrument of self-investi-
gation such as this inquiry needs?   Shall we

not here also be reduced to mere vagueness, to mere emotional appeals, or to those metaphysical arguments which are little more than disguised or regulated emotion? Is our psychology more than a mere descriptive system? Can the " introspective method " afford anything beyond an empirical knowledge of the processes of thought as they appear to the thinker? Or if we turn to psychophysiology, with its new promise of exact experiment, what do we get beyond such determinations of the rapidities and connections of nervous processes as merely prolong into the brain itself the analysis already applied to the operation of the organs of sense? Can either of these methods get down into the region where the answers to our real problems might perhaps be found?

No doubt the lessons of introspection are limited ; the lessons of objective experiment are as yet rudimentary. Yet in France at this moment psychology is in a more rapidly progressive, a more revolutionary condition than any other science whatever. It has so happened that to a new group of theoretical conceptions—namely, to the evolution doctrine,

as applied to mankind by Darwin, and the
psychical analysis of Spencer and Taine—has
been superadded a still newer group of psycho-
physiological observations and experiments:
the observations, namely, on hysteria and the
experiments in hypnotism of which Dr. Charcot's wards at the Salpêtrière form the most
celebrated centre.   We have here in psychology some kind of approach to a prediction
of small perturbations ; to something deeper
than the old-fashioned manual's sharp partition
of the sane mind and the insane ;—the sane
mind treated like some orrery unwinding itself
with diagrammatic regularity ; the insane mind
relegated to an inscrutable chaos.   Readers of
Dr. Hughlings-Jackson's "Croonian Lectures
on the Evolution and Dissolution of the
Nervous System" and similar tractates are of
course prepared for novel methods of analysis,
for the discovery of unsuspected lines of
cleavage amid the strata of mental operation.
But to the ordinary English reader such a
book, for instance, as Binet and Féré's Hand-
book of Hypnotism (miscalled Animal Magnet-
ism) in the *International Scientific Series* will
come with a string of surprises which will

almost suggest a mystification.   Yet Dr. Féré
is one of the most distinguished of rising French
physiologists ; M. Binet is a psychologist of
repute ; and the book is a quasi-official *résumé*
of the doctrines of the Salpêtrière school.
And if we take a somewhat wider view, I
believe that many Frenchmen will concur with
me in accounting the *Revue philosophique*, with
the Société de Psychologie physiologique (including MM. Taine, Charcot, Ribot, Richet,
Janet, Sully-Prudhomme, etc.), as perhaps the
most vital, the most distinctive nucleus of
modern French thought.[1]

   Yet even if this be so, and the strongest tide
of French speculation be now running in the
channel of experimental psychology, can we
expect that these specialised researches can
deeply influence men's general conception of
human fates ?   It is at least not easy to say
in what *other* way that general view is to be

---

[1] As I write these lines I observe in the *Revue des Deux Mondes*
for April 1 (1888) an article by Professor Paul Janet explaining
a very unusual step which has been taken by the authorities of
the Collège de France, "the transformation of the old traditional chair of Natural and International Law into a chair of
Experimental and Comparative Psychology."   Of the new
chair M. Ribot, the editor of the *Revue philosophique*, is the
first occupant.   See also Professor Janet's remarks (p. 549) on
the Société de Psychologie physiologique.

affected.   It will hardly be permanently altered by emotion, by rhetoric ; if modified at all, it must be modified by scientific discovery.   And if by scientific discovery, then why not by discovery in that which, if a science at all, is the highest of sciences ? In default of other revelations, *de cælo descendit* γνῶθι σεαυτόν.

In thus judging, we do but return to the doctrine of Socrates and Plato.   In their eyes man's knowledge of himself was the all-important, the light-bringing truth. The central question in Plato's philosophy—it must needs be a central question in all philosophies—was whether there exists in man a principle independent of the material universe. Plato supports his affirmative view partly by metaphysical arguments which, like most metaphysical arguments, have now passed out of date. But he supports it also by an argument based on actual, though insufficient, observation and experiment —namely, by the argument that our apparently intuitive recognition of geometrical truths and the like proves that we must have been already familiar with those truths in some previous existence. This special chain of reasoning seems now no longer valid. We explain " re-

miniscence " by heredity, or by the unconscious
generalisations of the child.   But Plato's method
of attacking the great problem on a side where
actual observation was possible—this was surely
eminently reasonable, eminently sound ; and
methods similar, but of greater potency, lie
ready to our hand to-day.

Of course, however, any discoveries which
can be thus reached by definite inquiry are
likely to be of modest dimensions as compared
to the large utterance of priest or prophet.
They may be significant ; they will scarcely be
overwhelming.   Personally, indeed, for reasons
which I shall not here repeat, but with which
some of my readers may be already acquainted,
I am disposed to think that such discoveries
are likely to prove highly favourable to human
hopes.   I do not attribute this view to the
psycho-physiological school of France.   Yet no
one who watches the vigour and rapidity of the
intellectual movement in which they are concerned can doubt that we are on the verge of
some considerable readjustment of our conceptions of the intimate nature of man.   And at
the same time it becomes every year more and
more difficult to conceive of a spiritual regener-

ation of France which shall start from an emotional, as opposed to a scientific, basis. Her educated classes, at least, seem equally insusceptible to old and to new forms of religious contagion. Catholicism seems to be slowly dying, but the "Religion of Humanity" was stillborn. And the moral fervour, the enthusiastic resignation, of a Clifford or a George Eliot amongst ourselves is replaced in a Taine or a Ribot by a tone of pure neutrality, as of men conscientiously analysing a Cosmos for which they are in no way responsible.

Let us hope that in this very neutrality there may be a certain element of advantage. Just as a Goncourt or a Maupassant may see certain facts of life the more lucidly on account of his detachment from moral interests, from moral dignity, so may the psycho-physiologists of France be aided in discovering some of the deeper elements in man's nature by dint of their very indifference to everything save the discovery itself.

In expressing these hopes, no doubt, we seem to be assuming that religion is essentially an affair of *knowledge*—the knowledge of those vital facts on which our general conception of

the universe must necessarily repose. And
this seems at variance with the view that
religion is essentially an affair of *faith*—the
clinging of the soul to the beliefs and ideals
which she feels as spiritually the highest. Yet
the two points of view are not radically inconsistent. Rather it may be said that faith in
this sense will always be indispensable ; but
that whereas in all ages a certain nucleus of
ascertained fact has been regarded as faith's
needful prerequisite, the only difference is that
in our own day so much of that ancient nucleus
has shrivelled away that some fresh accession
is needed before the flower of faith can spring
from it and shed fragrance on the unseen. And
to this quest of fresh *material for religion* the dis-
engaged temper of the French mind may contribute some added alertness, adaptability, power.

The position of this type of Frenchman may
perhaps be formulated as follows. " In the first
place," he would say, " I cannot respond to
stimuli addressed to my emotions alone. I
have had too many of such stimuli ; and after
the break-down of Catholicism, with its ancient
appeal and its majestic promises, I have no
appetite for the vague Theism, the austere

Stoicism, which are all that you can now offer me.   I see little reason to suppose that we survive death, or that life has a moral meaning ; and I cannot feel much enthusiasm for a world so incurably incomplete, so fundamentally un-just as our own.   Not that I am a fanatical pessimist ; I shall simply do my work, enjoy my pleasures, and think as little as may be about anything beyond.   At the same time I am quite aware that we are still at the begin-ning of our scientific knowledge of the universe and of man.   It is possible that you may discover something which will change my attitude.   You will not, I think, discover a God, or prove a moral government of the world. But short of that you may unearth some fact in man's nature which may make his destinies somewhat more hopeful, and a Providence somewhat less improbable than at present. Supposing——to take the extreme limit of what I can conceive you as proving——supposing that you could show me that I should survive death, I should certainly readjust my conceptions from top to bottom.   In that case I would produce emotions worthy of the occasion.   Meantime I shall keep them till they are really called for,

and shall pay no attention save to definite experiment, definite reasoning, addressed to problems
which do not lie plainly beyond the scope of
human intelligence, even though they may thus
far have wholly baffled human inquiry."

Somewhat in this fashion do the great
questions present themselves to minds no
longer prepossessed in favour of the Scheme of
Things.   The group of conceptions which we
call the universe—like the group of experiences
which we call human life—when viewed, as
Wordsworth says, "in disconnection dull and
spiritless," cease to impose themselves over-
whelmingly on the mind.   Their glory seems
unable to resist a gaze which analyses without
idealising ; and analysis without idealisation is
the very impulse and outcome of disenchanted
France.

I have now, though in a very brief and
imperfect way, accomplished the task which
seemed to me to have some promise of
instruction.   I have tried to decompose into its
constituent elements the vague but general
sense of *malaise* or decadence which permeates
so much of modern French literature and life.
And after referring this disenchantment to the

loss of certain beliefs and habits of thought
which the majority of educated Frenchmen
have come with more or less distinctness to
class as *illusions*, I have endeavoured—it may
be thought with poor success—to suggest some
possibility of the reconstitution of these illusions on a basis which can permanently resist
scientific attack.   In *experimental psychology* I
have suggested, so to say, a nostrum, but without propounding it as a panacea ; and I cannot
avoid the conclusion that we are bound to be
prepared for the worst.   Yet by "the worst"
I do not mean any catastrophe of despair,
any cosmic suicide, any world-wide unchain-
ing of the brute that lies pent in man.   I
mean merely the peaceful, progressive, orderly
triumph of *l'homme sensuel moyen ;* the gradual
adaptation of hopes and occupations to a purely
terrestrial standard : the calculated pleasures of
the cynic who is resolved to be a dupe no
more.

Such is the prospect from our tower of
augury—the warning note from France, whose
inward crises have so often prefigured the fates
through which Western Europe was to pass ere
long.   Many times, indeed, have declining

nations risen anew, when some fresh knowledge, some untried adventure, has added meaning and zest to life.   Let those men speak to us, if any there be, who can strengthen our hearts with some prevision happier than mine.   For if this vanward and eager people is never to be " begotten again unto a lively hope " by some energy still unfelt and unsuspected, then assuredly France will not suffer alone from her atrophy of higher life.   No ; in that case like causes elsewhere must produce like effects ; and there are other great nations whose decline will not be long delayed.

TENNYSON AS PROPHET
(1889)

> And we, the poor earth's dying race, and yet
> No phantoms, watching from a phantom shore
> Await the last and largest sense to make
> The phantom walls of this illusion fade,
> And show us that the world is wholly fair.
>
> *The Ancient Sage.*

THE aspect, the countenance of Lord Tennyson
—best rendered in Sir J. Millais' portrait, but
faithfully given also in many a photograph—
must often have struck his admirers with a
sense of surprise. It does not fit the popular
conception of him—a conception founded mainly
on his earlier work, and which presents him as
a refined, an idyllic poet, the chanter of love
and friendship, the adorner of half-barbarous
legends with a garb of tender grace. The faces
of other poets—of the ethereal Shelley, the
sensuous Keats, the passionate Byron, the be-
nignant Wordsworth—correspond well enough

to our notion of what they ought to be. But
Tennyson's face expresses not delicacy but
power ; it is grave even to sternness ; it is for-
midable in the sense which it gives of strength
and wisdom won through pain.

For indeed, both in aspect and in mood of
mind there has arisen between the poet of the
"Dream of Fair Women" and the poet of "Vastness " a change like the change between the poet
of *Comus* and the poet of *Samson Agonistes*.
In each case the potent nature, which in youth
felt keenlier than any contemporary the world's
beauty and charm, has come with age to feel
with like keenness its awful majesty, the clash
of unknown energies, and "the doubtful doom
of humankind." And the persistence of Lord
Tennyson's poetic gift in all its glory—a persistence scarcely rivalled since Sophocles—has
afforded a channel for the emergence of forces
which must always have lain deep in his nature,
but which were hidden from us by the very
luxuriance of the fancy and the emotion of
youth.

I would speak, then, of Tennyson as a *prophet*,
meaning by that term much more than a self-
inspired mystic, an eloquent visionary. I know

not how else to describe a service which humanity will always need.   Besides the *savant*,
occupied in discovering objective truth—besides
the artist occupied in representing and idealising
that truth—-we need some voice to speak to us
of those greatest, those undiscoverable things
which can never be wholly known but must
still less be wholly ignored or forgotten.   For
such a service we need something more than
orator or priest ; we need a sage, but a sage
whose wisdom is kindled with emotion, and
whose message comes to us with the authority
of a great personality, winged at once and
weighted by words of power.

Yet Tennyson's prophetic message has been
so delicately interwoven with his metrical and
literary charm, and has found, moreover, its
most potent expression in poems so recent in
date, that it has not often, I think, been
adequately recognised, or traced with due care
from its early to its later form.   There need,
therefore, I trust, be no presumption in an
attempt—for which the writer, of course, is
alone responsible—to arrange in clearer connection those weighty utterances which the
exigencies of art have scattered irregularly over

many pages, but which those who seek the
guidance of great minds must often desire to
reunite.

We have not here, indeed, a developed
system whose dogmas can be arranged in logical order. Rather may the reader be disposed
to say that there is no sure message ; that the
net result consists in hopes and possibilities
which the poet himself regards as transcending proof. Alas ! like the haul of living things
from the deep sea, the group of dogmas which
any mind brings up from the gulf of things
is apt to dwindle as the plummet sinks deeper
down ; and we have rather to ask, " Is there
at the bottom life at all ? " than to expect to
find our highly-organised creeds still flourish-
ing when we have plunged far into the dark
abyss.

This may sound but a cheerless saying, and
the Christian reader may perhaps complain
of a lack of explicit adhesion to Christian
doctrine in our representative poet. But I
would beg him to consider that the cause of
any creed, however definite, can hardly at present be better subserved than by indirect and
preliminary defences. I would remind him

that the Gospel story is not now supported, in
Paley's fashion, by insistence on its miracles
alone, but rather and mainly by subjective
arguments, by appeals to its intrinsic beauty
and probability, its adaptation to the instincts
and needs of men. Christianity assumes an
unseen world, and then urges that the life of
Christ is the fittest way in which such a world
could come into contact with the world we
know. The essential spirituality of the universe, in short, is the basis of religion, and it is
precisely this basis which is now assailed. In
former times the leading opponents of Christianity were mainly " Deists," and admitted in
some form or other a spiritual substratum for
visible things. Rousseau's irreducible minimum
of religion included a God and a future life.
But now the position is changed. The most
effective assailants of Christianity no longer
take the trouble to attack, as Voltaire did, the
Bible miracles in detail. They strike at the
root, and begin by denying—outright or virtually—that a spiritual world, a world beyond
the conceivable reach of mathematical formulæ,
exists for us at all. They say with Clifford that
" no intelligences except those of men and

animals have been at work in the solar system " ;
or, implying that the physical Cosmos is all,
and massing together all possible spiritual
entities under the name which most suggests
superstition, they affirm that the world " is
made of ether and atoms, and there is no room
for ghosts."

Now it is evident that unless this needful
preamble of any and every religion can be
proved—say rather unless the existence of an
unseen profounder world can be so presented
as to commend itself to our best minds as the
more likely hypothesis—it will be useless to
insist nowadays on the adaptation of any
given religion to the needs of the soul.   The
better adapted it is to man, the stronger will be
the presumption that it is a system created by
man—" the guess of a worm in the dust, and
the shadow of its desire."   It does not, of
course, follow that even were the existence of a
spiritual world demonstrated, any specific revelation of that world would be manifestly true.
But at any rate *unless* such a world be in some
sense believed in by the leading minds of the
race, no specific revelation whatever can permanently hold its ground.   If, therefore, certain

readers feel that Tennyson's championship is confined mainly to what they may regard as mere elements of Natural Religion, they need not on that account value him the less as a leader of the spiritual side of human thought. The work which he does may not be that which they most desire. But at least it is work indispensably necessary, if what they most desire is ever to be done. And they may reflect also that the Laureate's great predecessor did more for a spiritual view of the universe by his "Tintern Abbey" or his Platonic Ode than by his *Ecclesiastical Sonnets* or his pious hymn to St. Bees.

And first let us briefly consider the successive steps which mark Tennyson's gradual movement to his present position. They show, I think, an inward development coinciding with, or sometimes anticipating, the spiritual movement of the age. We may start with the "Supposed Confessions of a Second-rate Sensitive Mind"—a juvenile work, from whose title, for present purposes, we may perhaps omit the adjectives "supposed" and "second-rate." In this, the most agitated of all his poems, we find the soul urging onward

> Thro' utter dark a full-sail'd skiff,
> Unpiloted i' the echoing dance
> Of reboant whirlwinds ;—

and to the question " Why not believe, then ? "
we have as answer a simile of the sea which
cannot slumber like a mountain tarn, or

> Draw down into his vexèd pools
> All that blue heaven which hues and paves

the tranquil inland mere. Thus far there is
little that is distinctive, little beyond the
common experience of widening minds. But
in " The Two Voices " we have much that will
continue characteristic of Tennyson, and a
range of speculation not limited by Christian
tradition. Here we first encounter what may
be termed his most definite conjecture, to which
he returns in " De Profundis," and in the " Epi-
logue " which forms one of his latest works—
namely, the old Platonic hypothesis of the
multiform pre-existence of the soul. His
analogy from " trances " has received, I need
not say, much reinforcement from the experimental psychology of recent years.

> It may be that no life is found,
> Which only to one engine bound
> Falls off, but cycles always round.

> As old mythologies relate,
> Some draught of Lethe may await
> The slipping thro' from state to state.
>
> As here we find in trances, men
> Forget the dream that happens then,
> Until they fall in trance again.

There can be no doubt that any hypothesis of our survival of death must logically suggest our existence before earthly birth. Since, however, this latter hypothesis is not insisted on (though neither is it denied) by Christian orthodoxy, and has no quite obvious bearing on man's hopes and fears, it has dropped out of common thought, and its occurrence in individual speculation marks a certain disengagement and earnestness of inquiry.

The next main step is represented by *In Memoriam*; and in reading *In Memoriam* it is difficult to realise that the book was written by a young man, some half-century ago; so little is there, in all its range of thought and emotion, which the newest Science can condemn or the truest Religion find lacking. So sound an instinct has led the poet to dwell on the core of religion—namely, the survival of human love and human virtue—so genuine a candour has withheld him from insisting too positively on his own hopeful belief.   In spite of its sparse allusion to Christianity, *In Memoriam* has been widely accepted as a helpful companion to Christian devotion.   Is not this because the Christian feels that the survival of human love and virtue—however phrased or supported—is the essence of his Gospel too? that his good news is of the survival of a consummate love and virtue, manifested with the express object of proving that love and virtue *could* survive?

It is hardly too much to say that *In Memoriam* is the only speculative book of that epoch —epoch of the "Tractarian movement," and much similar "up-in-the-air balloon-work"— which retains a serious interest now.   Its brief cantos contain the germs of many a subsequent treatise, the indication of channels along which many a wave of opinion has flowed, down to that last "Philosophie der Erlösung," or Gospel of a sad Redemption—

> To drop head foremost in the jaws
> Of vacant darkness, and to cease—

which tacitly or openly is possessing itself of so many a modern mind.

Yet *In Memoriam*, in spite of all its preg-
nancy, hardly forms a part of what I have
called the prophetic message of Tennyson.
He still is feeling for Wisdom ; he has not
reached the point from whence he can speak
with confidence and power.

The first words, as I hold them, of the
message are presented, with characteristic
delicacy, in the form of a vision merely, and in
one of the least conspicuous poems.   The wife's
dream in " Sea Dreams " is an utterance of deep
import—the expression of a conviction that the
truth of things is good ; and that the resistless
force of truth, destroying one after another all
ancient creeds, and reaching at last to the fair
images of Virgin Mother and sinless Babe, is
nevertheless an impulse in harmony with the
best that those creeds contained ; and sheds a
mystic light on the ruined minsters, and mixes
its eternal music with the blind appeals of
men.

> But round the North, a light,
> A belt, it seem'd, of luminous vapour, lay,
> And ever in it a low musical note
> Swell'd up and died ; and, as it swell'd, a ridge
> Of breaker issued from the belt, and still
> Grew with the growing note, and when the note

> Had reach'd a thunderous fulness, on those cliffs
> Broke, mixt with awful light (the same as that
> Living within the belt) whereby she saw
> That all those lines of cliffs were cliffs no more,
> But huge cathedral fronts of every age,
> Grave, florid, stern, as far as eye could see,
> One after one : and then the great ridge drew,
> Lessening to the lessening music, back,
> And past into the belt and swell'd again
> Slowly to music : ever when it broke
> The statues, king or saint, or founder fell.

But here the subtlest point is that the very lamentations of those who regret this ruin are themselves part and parcel of the same harmonious impulse—

> Their wildest wailings never out of tune
> With that sweet note

to which the ancient images are crumbling down, and the resistless wave advancing from a luminous horizon of the sea.

Where, then, are we to look for a revelation of the secret which, broadening from its far belt of light, is to overwhelm the limited and evanescent phases of human faith?

The nearest approach to a statement of creed in Tennyson's poems is to be found in a few stanzas which he read at the first meeting

of the Metaphysical Society, the group of
thinkers mentioned in his sonnet on the inception of the Review in which these pages first
appeared :—

The sun, the moon, the stars, the seas, the hills and
the plains—
Are not these, O Soul, the Vision of Him who
reigns ?

Is not the Vision He ? tho' He be not that which He
seems ?
Dreams are true while they last, and do we not live
in dreams ?

Earth, these solid stars, this weight of body and
limb,
Are they not sign and symbol of thy division from
Him ? . . .

Speak to Him thou for He hears, and Spirit with
Spirit can meet—
Closer is He than breathing, and nearer than hands
and feet. . . .

And the ear of man cannot hear, and the eye of man
cannot see ;
But if we could see and hear, this Vision—were it
not He ?

In the " Higher Pantheism " of these familiar
lines, the reader accustomed to the study of
religions will seem to recognise that we have

come to the end of the story. We have reached
the end of Oriental religion, the end of Greek ;
we stand where stood Plotinus, fusing into a
single ecstasy every spiritual emotion of that
ancient world.

But to see and to have seen that Vision is reason
no longer, but more than reason, and before reason,
and after reason ; as also is that Vision which is seen.
And perchance we should not speak of *sight*. For
that which is seen—if we must needs speak of the
Seer and the Seen as twain and not as one—that
which is seen is not discerned by the seer nor conceived by him as a second thing ; but, becoming as
it were other than himself, he of himself contributeth
nought, but as when one layeth centre upon centre
he becometh God's and one with God. Wherefore this
vision is hard to tell of. For how can a man tell of
that as other than himself, which when he discerned
it seemed not other, but one with himself indeed ?[1]

Or take again the words of Arthur at the end
of the " Holy Grail "—the spiritually central
passage, so to say, in all the *Idylls of the King*—
when the king describes the visions of the night
or of the day which come when earthly work is
done—

> In moments when he feels he cannot die,
> And knows himself no vision to himself,
> Nor the high God a vision ;

---

[1] Plotinus, *Enn.* vi. 10.

and compare this with any one of the passages
where Plotinus endeavours in halting speech to
reproduce those moments of unison whose
memory brightens his arid argument with oases
of a lucid joy.

And it may be that this was not vision, but some
other manner of sight, ay, an ecstasy and a simplicity
and a self-surrender, and a still passion of contact
and of unison, when that which is within the Holy
Place is discerned. . . . And falling from that sight
if he arouse again the virtue in him, and perceive
himself wholly adorned, he shall be lifted up once
more; through Virtue looking upon Mind and through
Wisdom upon very God.   Thus is the life of blessed
gods and of godlike men a renunciation of earthly
joy, a deliverance from earthly sorrow, a flight of the
One to the One.

To some such point as this, as I have said,
the instinct of reverence, the emotion of holiness,
must tend to lead souls to such emotions born.
And in former times this mystical standpoint
seemed in some sense independent of controversy.   Historical criticism on the Gospels,
geological disproof of the Mosaic cosmogony,
scarcely rose into that thinner air.   But the
assault now made is more paralysing, more
fundamental.   For it is based on formulæ
which are in a certain sense demonstrable, and

which seem to embrace the whole extent of
things. The Cosmos, we now say, is a system
of ether and atoms, in which the sum of matter
and the sum of energy are constant quantities.
And the Cosmos is the scene of universal evolution, according to unchangeable law. Hence
it seems to follow that no human soul or will
can add a fresh energy of its own ; that there
can be nothing but a ceaseless transformation
of force, which would proceed in just the same
way were all consciousness to be removed from
the automata who fancy that they direct the
currents along which they inevitably flow. It
seems to follow, too, that even the highest of
these automata have been brought into a
momentary existence by no Heavenly Father,
no providential scheme ; but in the course of a
larger and unconscious process, which in itself
bears no relation to human happiness or virtue.

As all this begins to be dimly realised, men
may be seen, like ants in a trodden ant-hill,
striving restlessly to readjust their shattered
conceptions. It is borne in upon them that the
traditional optimism of Western races may be
wholly illusory ; that human life may indeed,
as the East has held, be on the whole an evil,

and man's choice lie between a dumb resignation and that one act of rebellion which makes
at least an end.   And thus, in an age little given
to metaphysic, we find pessimistic systems more
vigorous than any other, and the intellect of
France, Russia, Germany deeply honeycombed
with a tacit despair.

But though pessimism may spread among
the thoughtful, it cannot possibly be the practical creed of progressive peoples.   They must
maintain their energy by some kind of compromise between old views and new ; and the
compromises which we see around us, though
at war among themselves, are yet the offspring
of the same need, and serve to break, at different
points, the terrible transition.   There is the
movement which began with Broad-Churchism,
and which seems now to broaden further into a
devotion to Christ which altogether repudiates
the Resurrection on which His first followers
based His claim to be the bringer of a true
Gospel rather than the most mistaken of all
enthusiasts.   And a few steps farther from old
beliefs stands that other compromise known as
Positivism—a religion consisting simply in the
resolute maintenance of the traditional opti-

mistic view when the supposed facts that made
for optimism have all been abandoned. Never
have we come nearer to " the grin without the
cat " of the popular fairy tale than in the
brilliant paradoxes with which some kindly
rhetorician—himself steeped in deserved prosperity—would fain persuade us that all in this
sad world is well, since Auguste Comte has
demonstrated that the effect of our deeds lives
after us, so that what we used to call eternal
death—the cessation, in point of fact, of our
own existence — may just as well be con-
sidered as eternal life of a very superior
description.

But although these and similar compromises
are only too open to the pessimist's attack, one
may well hesitate as to whether it is right or
desirable to assail them. Should we not en-
courage any illusion which will break the fall,
and repeat in favour of these fragile substitutes
the same reticence which it so long seemed well
to use in criticising Christianity itself?

Such, at any rate, is not Lord Tennyson's
attitude in the matter. In his view, it seems,
these blanched survivals of optimism may be
brushed aside without scruple. He is not afraid

to set forth a naked despair as the inevitable outcome of a view of the world which omits a moral government or a human survival. A grave responsibility, which the clear-seeing poet would scarcely have undertaken, had not his own confidence in the happier interpretation been strong and assured.

His presentation of absolute hopelessness is put in the mouth of a man undergoing one of those seasons of unmerited anguish which are the real, the intimate problem with which any religion or any philosophy has to deal.

" A man and his wife, having lost faith in a God, and hope of a life to come "—so run the prefatory words to " Despair "—" and being utterly miserable in this, resolve to end themselves by drowning. The woman is drowned, but the man rescued by a minister of the sect he had abandoned ; "—and to this minister he describes the reflections of that which had so nearly been his own last hour.

And first of all, and prompting to the suicidal act, was the passion of pity for himself and all mankind—the feeling that there was no hope or remedy except that last plunge into the dark.

L

But pity—the Pagan held it a vice—was in her and
    in me,
Helpless, taking the place of the pitying God that
    should be !
Pity for all that aches in the grasp of an idiot power,
And pity for our own selves on an earth that bore not
    a flower ;
Pity for all that suffers on land or in air or the deep,
And pity for our own selves till we long'd for eternal
    sleep.

" It seems to me," says the character in
which one of the ablest of our younger writers
has expressed her own inward battle, " it seemed
to me as if I saw, mysteriously, a new Satan, a
rebel angel of good, raising his banners against
the Jehovah of Evil ; a creature like Franken-
stein's image, a terrible new kind of monster,
more noble than its base maker." [1]   How shall
a man avoid such indignant compassion as this ?
Let him face his own doom bravely as he may,
how shall he look complacently on the anguish
of others, knowing that for their forlornness
there is no pity anywhere save such thin stream
as he and his like can give ? that there lives,
perhaps, no creature wiser or more helpful than
himself in the star-sown fields of heaven ?

[1] *Baldwin*, by Vernon Lee, p. 124.

And the suns of the limitless Universe sparkled and
    shone in the sky,
Flashing with fires as of God, but we knew that their
    light was a lie—
Bright as with deathless hope—but, however they
    sparkled and shone,
The dark little worlds running round them were worlds
    of woe like our own—
No soul in the heaven above, no soul on the earth
    below,
A fiery scroll written over with lamentation and woe.

" The starry heavens without ; the moral law
within " : with what an irony must that old
formula of august hope strike on a mind like
this ! " The moral law within " : the inherited
instincts which have made my tribe successful
among its neighbour tribes, but which simply
fail and have no further meaning in this my
solitary extremest hour ! " The starry heavens
without " : appalling spectacle of aimless immensity ! inconceivable possibilities of pain !
vastness of a Universe which knows not of
our existence and could not comprehend our
prayer !

O we poor orphans of nothing—alone on that lonely
    shore—
Born of the brainless Nature who knew not that which
    she bore !

The man and wife bid farewell to each other
as the water rises round them.

Ah God, should we find Him, perhaps, perhaps, if we
    died, if we died ;
We never had found Him on earth, this earth is a
    fatherless Hell—
"Dear Love, for ever and ever, for ever and ever
    farewell,"
Never a cry so desolate, not since the world began,
Never a kiss so sad, no, not since the coming of man!

A comparison of these lines with the lines
in the " Palace of Art " where Tennyson, still a
young man, has painted the soul's last distress,
will show how far more awful the world-problem
reflected in the poet's mind has become since
that earlier day.   In the " Palace of Art " the soul
which has lived for her own pleasure alone feels
herself " exilèd from eternal God," severed like
a land-locked pool from the mighty movement
of all things " toward one sure goal."   It is an
agony of remorse and terror, but it carries with
it a germ of hope.   There *is* the goal towards
which the universe is striving.   There *is* the
eternal God.   And after repentance and pur-
gation the erring soul can hope to renew the
sacred sympathies, and to rejoin the advancing
host.

On the other hand the woe described in
"Despair" deepens where that other sorrow found
its dawn.   There is absolutely nothing to which
effort can be directed, or appeal can lie.   It is
no longer conceivable that any soul, by any
action or passion, can alter the immutable
destiny which hangs blindly over all.

Yet I must not speak as if those who deem
human survival a superfluous consolation had
made no effort to meet such crises as that on
which Tennyson dwells.   I quote a well-known
passage in which Clifford has depicted the
"unseen helper" who may be looked for when
no other help is nigh.

> He who, wearied or stricken in the fight with
> the powers of darkness, asks himself in a solitary
> place, "Is it all for nothing? shall we indeed be over-
> thrown?" he does find something which may justify
> that thought [of an unseen helper of men].   In such a
> moment of utter sincerity, when a man has bared his
> own soul before the immensities and the eternities,
> a presence in which his own poor personality is
> shrivelled into nothingness, arises within him, and
> says, as plainly as words can say, "I am with thee, and
> I am greater than thou." . . . The dim and shadowy
> outlines of the superhuman Deity fade slowly away
> from before us ; and as the mist of his presence floats
> aside, we perceive with greater and greater clearness
> the shape of a yet grander and nobler figure—of Him

who made all Gods and shall unmake them.   From
the dim dawn of history, and from the inmost depth
of every soul, the face of our father Man looks out
upon us with the fire of eternal youth in his eyes,
and says, " Before Jehovah was, I am ! "

Yet would one not be in danger of observing
that the face of this summarised or composite
ancestor was of somewhat too simian a type ?
Might not "the fire of youth in his eyes"
suggest unpleasantly that he had called his
descendants into being for reasons quite other
than a far-seeing desire that they should suffer
and be strong ?   And if Jehovah and all gods
be his fable and his fiction, does that make him
a whit more strong to save ?

Why should we bear with an hour of torture, a
    moment of pain,
If every man die for ever, if all his griefs are in vain,
And the homeless planet at length will be wheel'd thro'
    the silence of space,
Motherless evermore of an ever-vanishing race,
When the worm shall have writhed its last, and its last
    brother-worm will have fled
From the dead fossil skull that is left in the rocks of
    an earth that is dead ?

" What is it to me," said Marcus Aurelius, " to
live in a world without a Providence ? "   " I live,"

said Prince Bismarck in 1878, "a life of great
activity, and occupy a lucrative post; but all
this could offer me no inducement to live one
day longer, did I not believe in God and a better
future." It is well to quote men like these when
one sees the words "morbid" and "unmanly,"
taking in the Positivist Camp the place which
the words "dangerous" and "unsound" have
occupied so long in orthodox polemics. It is
not clear why it should be unmanly to face the
bitter as well as the sweet; to see life in a dry
light, tinted neither by the sunset rays of a
vanishing Paradise, nor by the silvery moon-
light of a philosopher's dream.

In Tennyson's view, at any rate, this delibe-
rate rejection of human life as meaningless
without a future is not the mere outcome of
such misery as that of the spokesman in
"Despair." It forms the theme of one of his last
and most majestic personal utterances, of that
poem of "Vastness," which one may place beside
the choruses in the *Œdipus at Colonus*, as illus-
trations, the one of an old man's wisdom in all
its benignity, the other of an old man's wisdom
in all its authority and power.

The insignificance of human life, if moral

evolution be for ever checked by death, is no
new theme ; but it is here enforced as though
by Plato's " spectator of all time and of all existence," with a range of view which sees one
man's death recall or prefigure, not, as Dido's,
the fall only of Tyre or Carthage, but the de-
solation of entire planets, and the evanescence
of unknown humanities in dispeopled fields of
Heaven.   Seen with that cosmic gaze, earth's
good and evil alike seem the illusions of a
day.

Many a hearth upon our dark globe sighs after many
    a vanish'd face,
Many a planet by many a sun may roll with the dust
    of a vanish'd race.

Raving politics, never at rest—as this poor earth's
    pale history runs—
What is it all but a trouble of ants in the gleam of a
    million million of suns ? . . .

Stately purposes, valour in battle, glorious annals of
    army and fleet,
Death for the right cause, death for the wrong cause,
    trumpets of victory, groans of defeat ; . . .

Pain, that has crawl'd from the corpse of Pleasure, a
    worm which writhes all day, and at night
Stirs up again in the heart of the sleeper, and stings
    him back to the curse of the light ; . . .

Love for the maiden crown'd with marriage, no regrets
    for aught that has been,
Household happiness, gracious children, debtless
    competence, golden mean ; . . ヽ ·

What is it all, if we all of us end but in being our own
    corpse-coffins at last,
Swallow'd in Vastness, lost in Silence, drown'd in the
    deeps of a meaningless Past ?

What but a murmur of gnats in the gloom, or a
    moment's anger of bees in their hive ?—

    *   *   *   *

Peace, let it be ! for I loved him, and love him for
    ever : the dead are not dead but alive.

How else than thus can we now imagine the cosmic position of man ? We have long ceased to think of him as standing on an immutable earth, with sun and stars revolving round his central home. Nor can we any longer fancy him, as Comte used to fancy him, housed in the snug security of his solar system ; —an unroofed and fenceless plot, from whence every moment the irrecoverable sun-rays tremble out into the blackness and are squandered in the gulf of heaven. We must regard him with foresight of his end ; with such comfort only as we may find in the thought that other races, powerless as he, may have been shaped, and may yet be shaped, from the like clash of atoms,

for the like history and the like doom. Let
these cry aloud if they will into the interstellar
spaces, and call it prayer ; they hear not each
other, and there is none else to hear.   For in
this infinity love and virtue have no share ; they
are of all illusions the most fragile, derivative,
evanescent ; they have no part or lodgment in
the fixed reality of things.

And yet this prospect, which is slowly im-
posing itself as inevitable, is in reality but a
conjecture like all the rest.   Such, we may admit, must be the universe if it be reducible to
ether and atoms alone ; if life and consciousness
be its efflorescence and not its substratum, and
that which was from the beginning be the
lowest and not the highest of all.   But in truth
a reduction of the Cosmos into ether and atoms
is scarce more reasonable than its reduction
into the four elements, air, water, earth, and fire.
The ancients boldly assumed that the world
was made of things which our senses can reach.
The modern *savant* too often tacitly implies
that the world is made of things which our
calculations can reach.   Yet this is still a disguised, a mediate anthropomorphism.   There is
no reason to assume that our calculations, any

more than our senses, have cognisance of any large fraction of the events which are occurring even in our own region of time and space. The notion that we have now attained to a kind of outline sketch of the universe is not really consistent with the very premises on which it is based. For on those premises our view must inevitably have limits depending on nothing wider than the past needs of living organisms on this earth. We have acquired, presumably, a direct perception of such things as it has helped our ancestors most to perceive during their struggle for existence ; and an indirect perception of such other things as we have been able to infer from our group of direct perceptions. But we cannot limit the entities or operations which may coexist, even in our part of the Cosmos, with those already known. The universe may be infinite in an infinite number of ways.

Considerations such as these are not formally disputed, but they are constantly ignored. In spite of the continued hints which nature gives us to enlarge our conceptions in all kinds of unlooked-for ways, the instinct of system, of a rounded and completed doctrine, is apt to be too strong for us, and a determined protest

against premature synthesis is as much needed
now as ever.   Such protest may naturally take
one of two forms.   It may consist of a careful
registration of residual phenomena in all directions, which the current explanations fail to
include.   Or it may consist—and this is the
prophet's task—of imaginative appeal, impress-
ive assertion of the need of a profounder insight and a wider purview before we quit our
expectant attitude, and act as though apparent
limitations were also real, or the universe
fathomed in any of its dimensions by human
perception and power.   It is in this mood that
Tennyson draws from the standing mystery of
a child's birth the conception of a double, a
synchronous evolution ; of a past which has
slowly shaped the indwelling spirit as well as
the fleshly habitation.   First comes the physical
ancestry :—

> Out of the deep, my child, out of the deep,
> Where all that was to be, in all that was,
> Whirl'd for a million æons thro' the vast
> Waste dawn of multitudinous-eddying light.

For thus does the baby's structure remount to
the primordial nebula ; the atoms of its hand
have been volleyed for inconceivable ages

through far-off tracts of gloom, and have passed
through a myriad combinations, inanimate and
animate, to become the child's for a moment,
and to speed once more away.

> Out of the deep, my child, out of the deep,
> From that great deep, before our world begins,
> Whereon the Spirit of God moves as he will—
> Out of the deep, my child, out of the deep,
> From that true world within the world we see,
> Whereof our world is but the bounding shore.

For thus an invisible world may antecede the
visible, and an inconceivable world the conceivable; while yet we ourselves, here and
now, are living equally in both; though our
spirit be beclouded by its " descent into generation "; which, in Plotinus' words, is " a fall, a
banishment, a moulting of the wings of the
soul."

> O dear Spirit half-lost
> In thine own shadow and this fleshly sign
> That thou art thou—who wailest being born
> And banish'd into mystery, and the pain
> Of this divisible-indivisible world
> Among the numerable-innumerable
> Sun, sun, and sun, thro' finite-infinite space
> In finite-infinite Time—our mortal veil
> And shatter'd phantom of that infinite One,
> Who made thee unconceivably Thyself
> Out of His whole World-self and all in all.

Is there, then, any hint of a possibility of transcending these contradictory inconceivables? of re-attaining the clearness which is blurred and confused by the very fact of our individuation ? of participating in that profounder consciousness which, in Tennyson's view, is not the "epiphenomenon" but the root and reality of all ?

A passage in the "Ancient Sage," known to be based upon the poet's own experience, describes some such sensation of resumption into the universal, following upon a self-induced ecstasy.

> And more, my son! for more than once when I
> Sat all alone, revolving in myself
> The word that is the symbol of myself,
> The mortal limit of the Self was loosed,
> And past into the Nameless, as a cloud
> Melts into Heaven. I touch'd my limbs, the limbs
> Were strange not mine—and yet no shade of doubt,
> But utter clearness, and thro' loss of Self
> The gain of such large life as match'd with ours
> Were Sun to spark—unshadowable in words,
> Themselves but shadows of a shadow-world.

This passage raises in the directest form a question which becomes ever more vitally important as external systems of theology crumble

away.   Can ecstasy ever be a state higher than
normal life, or is it always referable to delusion
or disease?   Now it is undoubted that the
great majority of states of true ecstasy which
are now observed occur in hysterical patients,
as one phase of a complex attack.   The
temptation to rank ecstasy on much the same
level with hysterical spasm or mutism is naturally irresistible.   And yet, as I have urged
elsewhere, this is by no means a safe conclusion.   A hysterical fit indicates a lamentable
instability of the nervous system.   But it is by
no means certain, *à priori*, that every symptom
of that instability, without exception, will be of
a degenerative kind.   The nerve-storm, with
its unwonted agitations, may possibly lay bare
some deep-lying capacity in us which could
scarcely otherwise have come to light.   Recent
experiments on both sensation and memory in
certain abnormal states have added plausibility
to this view, and justify us in holding that, in
spite of its frequent association with hysteria,
ecstasy is not necessarily in itself a morbid
symptom.

And if we can allow ourselves to look at
ecstasy apart from its associations with hysteria

and fanaticism—as it is presented to us, say,
by Plato or Wordsworth, or, in more developed
form (as we have seen), by Tennyson or Plotinus
—then, assuredly, it is a phenomenon which
cannot be neglected in estimating man's actual
or nascent powers of arriving at a knowledge
of truth. " Great wit and madness " are both of
them divergences from the common standard ;
but the study of genius may have as much to
teach us of the mind's evolution as the study of
insanity has to teach us of its decay.

And, moreover, if indeed, as Tennyson has
elsewhere suggested, and as many men now
believe, there exist some power of communication between human minds without sensory
agency—

> Star to star vibrates light ; may soul to soul
> Strike thro' some finer element of her own ?—

then surely it would be in accordance with
analogy that these centres of psychical perception should be immersed in a psychical
continuum, and that their receptivity should
extend to influences of larger than human
scope. And if so, then the obscure intuitions
which have made the vitality of one religion

after another may have discerned confusedly
an ultimate fact, a fact deeper than any law
which man's mind can formulate, or any creed
to which his heart can cling. For these things,
to whatever purport, were settled long ago ;
they must be the great structural facts of the
Cosmos, determined before our Galaxy shaped
itself or souls first entered into man.

Enough, perhaps, has been said to indicate
the aspect in which this great poet's teaching
—in itself, no doubt, many-sided, and transcending the grasp of any single disciple—has
presented itself to at least one student, who has
spared no pains to follow it. As here conceived, it is a teaching which may well outlast
our present confusion and struggle. For
Tennyson is the prophet simply of a Spiritual
Universe : the proclaimer of man's spirit as
part and parcel of that Universe, and indestructible as the very root of things. And
in these beliefs, though science may not prove
them, there is nothing which can conflict with
science ; for they do but assert in the first
place that the universe is infinite in more ways
than our instruments can measure ; in the
second place that evolution, which is the law

M

for the material universe, is the law for virtue
as well.   It is not on interference but on
analogy, not on catastrophe but on completion,
that they base the foundation of hope.   More
there may be — truths holier, perhaps, and
happier still ; but should not *these* truths, if
true they be, suffice for man ?   Is it not
enough to give majesty to the universe, purpose and dignity to life, if he can once believe
that his upward effort—what he here calls
virtue—shall live and persist for ever ?   " Give
her the glory of going on, and still to be."

If there are some who will deem this hope
insufficient, there are many more among the
disciples of science who will smile at it as an
unprovable dream.   For my own part, too, I
believe that the final answer—and this I say in
no unhopeful spirit—must depend on the discoveries of Science herself.   " We are ancients
of the earth " ; and if there be indeed an unseen
world we assuredly need not imagine that we
have yet exhausted our means of discovering
it.   But meantime we more than ever need our
prophets ; and the true poet comes nearer to
inspiration than any prophet to whom we can
hope to listen now.   Let his intuitions come

to us dissolved in that fusion of thought and
melody which makes the highest art we know ;
let flashes of a strange delight——" like sparkles
in the stone avanturine "——reveal at once the
beauty and the darkness of the meditations
whence the song has sprung. Give us, if so it
may be, the exaltation which lifts into a high
community ; the words which stir the pulse like
passion, and wet the eyes like joy, and with
the impalpable breath of an inward murmur
can make a sudden glory in the deep of the
heart. Give us——but who shall give it ? or
how in days like these shall not the oracles
presently be dumb ?

In Tennyson and Browning we have veritable fountain-heads of the spiritual energy of
our time. "Ranging and ringing thro' the
minds of men," their words are linked in many
a memory with what life has held of best.
But these great poets have passed already the
common term of man ; and when we look to
the pair whose genius might have marked them
as successors, we see too clearly the effect of
this "dimness of our vexation" upon sensitive
and generous souls. The "singer before sun-
rise "——capable of so quick a response to all

chivalrous ardours—has turned his face from
the vaster problems, has given himself to literature as literature, and to poetry as art alone.
And he, again, who dwelt with so ravishing a
melancholy on Eld and Death, whose touch
shall shrivel all human hope and joy,—he has
felt that every man may well grasp with hasty
eagerness at delights which so soon pass by for
all, and has followed how incoherent an ideal
along how hazardous a way !

It seems sometimes as though poetry, which
has always been half art, half prophecy, must
needs abandon her higher mission ; must turn
only to the bedecking of things that shall
wither and the embalming of things that shall
decay.   She will speak, as in the *Earthly
Paradise*, to listeners

> laid upon a flowery slope
> 'Twixt inaccessible cliffs and unsailed sea ;

and behind all her utterance there will be an
awful reticence, an unforgotten image of the
end.   How, then, will Tennyson's hopes and
visions sound to men, when his living utterance
has fallen silent, like the last oracle in the
Hellenic world?   I can imagine that our descend-

ants may shun the message whose futile confidence will add poignancy to their despair.   Or,
on the other hand, if indeed the Cosmos make
for good, and evolution be a moral as well as a
material law, will men in time avail to prove
it ?   For then they will look back on Tennyson
as no belated dreamer, but as a leader who in
the darkest hour of the world's thought would
not despair of the destiny of man.   They will
look back on him as Romans looked back on
that unshaken Roman who purchased at its
full price the field of Cannæ, on which at that
hour victorious Hannibal lay encamped with
his Carthaginian host.

MODERN POETS AND COSMIC LAW

1893

> But earth's dark forehead flings athwart the heavens
> Her shadow crown'd with stars—and yonder—out
> To northward—some that never set, but pass
> From sight and night to lose themselves in day.
> I hate the black negation of the bier,
> And wish the dead, as happier than ourselves
> And higher, having climb'd one step beyond
> Our village miseries, might be borne in white
> To burial or to burning, hymn'd from hence
> With songs in praise of death, and crown'd with flowers!
> *The Ancient Sage.*

WORDSWORTH, Darwin, Tennyson,—the three greatest Englishmen of our century,—all now have passed away. *Greatest* I call them, not for personal faculties alone, which are hard to compare as between the many men of genius whom our age has produced, but because it seems to me that these men's faculties have achieved most in the most important directions, in the intuition, discovery, promulgation of fundamental cosmic law. And by cosmic law I here mean not such rules merely as may hold good universally for matter, or motion, or abstract quantities, but principles which, even if as yet but dimly and narrowly understood, may conceivably be valid for the whole universe, on all possible planes of being. Of such principles, we have as yet but three ; —Uniformity, Conservation, Evolution. We believe that all operations in the universe obey unchanging law. We believe that all matter and all energy known to us are indestructible. And we believe that all physical and vital operation in the universe is at present following certain obscurely discernible streams of tendency, whose source and goal are alike unknown. The first of these laws lies at the root of all Science ; the second at the root of Physics ; the third at the root of Biology.

It is not, of course, with any one of these three laws that the work of Wordsworth or of Tennyson is connected. Of a *fourth* cosmic principle, to which, as I hold, they have helped to introduce mankind, there will be mention later on. Meantime my purpose is briefly to review the work of Tennyson and of our two great poets who survive—Browning I must omit for want of space—in reference to its most serious or philosophical import.[1]   And such criticism, if it is to have any real value, must needs start thus *ab ovo*, and must take account of the speculative or ethical standpoint from which each poet writes.   Nor can such standpoint be any longer indicated by words which merely express inclusion or non-inclusion among the adherents of any definite form of faith.

For the change which is coming over our questionings of the universe affects the poet not less intimately, if less directly, than it affects the *savant* or the philosopher.   The conceptions which he breathes in from the intellectual atmosphere are no longer traditional, but scientific ; no longer catastrophic, but evolutionary ; no longer planetary, but cosmical.   He may still feel that certain facts in human history have had a unique importance for man.   But he must recognise that in order to understand those very facts we must endeavour to understand the universe around us.   That

---

[1] In thus continuing, after the poet's death, the argument begun, in the essay just preceding, during his lifetime, I may say that I have reason to believe that the line there taken, based in part upon his own conversation, was not unacceptable to Lord Tennyson.

universe cannot have changed appreciably in
two thousand years. Taking it as a whole,
what was going on then must be going on now.

Yet if the poet endeavours to nourish himself
on cosmical laws, he soon finds how ill-suited
they are for the sustenance of the human heart.
They are the offspring, not of philosophical
musing or generous emotion, but of observations,
experiments, computations, conducted with an
entire absence of ethical preoccupation. Imperfectly understood in themselves, they are yet
more difficult to translate into formulæ which
will answer the questions that we most wish to
ask. Does the law of the uniformity of Nature
cancel all that has been held as miracle or
revelation, or may so-called miracle and
revelation themselves form a stable element in
the succession of cause and effect? Does the
law of the conservation of energy condemn
man's consciousness to extinction when the
measurable energies which build up his chemical
texture pass back into the inorganic world, or
may his conscious life be a form of activity
which, just because it is not included in our
cycle of mutually transformable energies, is
itself in its own proper form as imperishable as

they ?   What does evolution mean, when we get below the obviously superficial terms in which we now describe it as progressing from the simple to the complex, from the homogeneous to the heterogeneous, and the like ? Does it apply to the moral, or only to the material world ?   In its application to the material world, is it in any sense continuous and eternal, or is it always temporary and truncated, as must needs be the case with our planetary and solar evolution, and may conceivably be the case with all the stellar evolution which we perceive or infer ?   And if it applies to the moral future of mankind, is it truncated there also, as must be the case if man exists only while he can inhabit the surface of a planet which, at the best, is only warranted habitable for a few million years ? or has it the continuity and eternity for which man's personal immortality alone would offer scope ?

And broadly, if the alien and impersonal character of all these laws convinces us that the universe is in no way constructed to meet the moral needs of man, can we then discern its purport ? — is any effort possible to us, or must we drift helplessly with the cosmic stream ?

It so happens that the respective attitudes of Mr. Swinburne and Mr. William Morris towards these fundamental problems are specially interesting in two opposite ways—with Mr. Swinburne, from his extraordinary intellectual detachment from the ordinary emotions of humanity ; with Mr. Morris from the intensity with which he personally shares those emotions.

Mr. Swinburne's case is a very unusual one. His temperament, it need hardly be said, is one of exceptional keenness and fervour ; but he has himself explained that this fervour is elicited mainly by poetry and by the aspects of Nature. The name which the poet assumes in his principal autobiographical poem, "Thalassius," or Child of the Sea,—like the symbolical parentage of the Sun-God which he assigns to himself,—is significant of a nature for which these elemental relationships rank as primary passions, and which finds its intensest stimulus in flooding light and stormy ocean. Not, of course, that a temperament so vivid has wholly escaped strong personal feeling. Thalassius describes both a sad experience of love, and also a period of reckless wandering, "by many a vine-leafed, many a rose-hung road." But

from this wandering he feels, in his allegory,
the Sea, his mother, recall him,

And charm him from his own soul's separate sense
With infinite and invasive influence,
That made strength sweet in him and sweetness
    strong,
Being now no more a singer, but a song.

To no poet, perhaps, was this last line ever
more justly applicable. The idea is further
developed in a passage from " On the Cliffs,"
where the poet addresses the nightingale,—in
whom also the intensity and volume of song seem
to transcend the actual personal emotion :—

We were not made for sorrow, thou and I,
For joy nor sorrow, sister, were we made,
To take delight and grief to live or die,
Assuaged by pleasures and by pains affrayed,
That melt men's hearts or alter; we retain
A memory mastering pleasure and all pain,
A spirit within the sense of ear and eye,
A soul behind the soul, that seeks and sings,
And makes our life move only with its wings.

The essential isolation—the view of life as
from without—which follows on this character,
is described in " Thalassius " :—

From no loved lips and on no loving breast
Have I sought ever for such gifts as bring
Comfort, to stay the secret soul to sleep.

The joys, the loves, the labours, whence men reap
Rathe fruit of hopes and fears,
I have made not mine ; the best of all my days
Have been as those fair fruitless summer strays,—
Those waterwaifs which but the sea-wind steers,—
Glad flakes of foam and flowers on footless ways
Which take the wind in season and the sun,
And when the wind wills is their season done.

One marked element of the poet's youthful
training has not yet been mentioned. This
was the influence of Walter Savage Landor ;
—an influence pointing mainly towards the
worship of Liberty. And it is well for the
world that this early bias was implanted, and
that in after years the last of "the world's
saviours "—the representative, for poetry even
more than for history, of the last great struggle
where all chivalrous sympathies could range
themselves undoubtingly on one side—should
have received a crown of song such as had
scarcely before been laid at the feet of any
living hero. But since Mazzini's work was
done, there has been no struggle which has
called forth the poet's sympathy with equal
clearness. "Republic" was a word with which
he was wont to conjure ; but we have just seen
one of the three largest empires of the world

turned into a republic without producing a stanza from Mr. Swinburne, or indeed any appreciable result except a fall in stocks.

The fact is that, fortunately for mankind, Liberty is becoming a matter for the statesman to define rather than for the poet to invoke; and that the denunciation of tyranny is falling into the same obsolescence which has already overtaken the glorification of personal prowess as a theme of song. The youths who bore their swords in myrtles are almost as remote from us now as the youth who dragged his enemy round the walls of Troy. We thrill to the old music; but that *motif* can be worked afresh no more. Liberty represents the next stage of progress after Peace and Plenty; when men, having attained by forceful government to security of property, are inevitably urged by the mere weight of multitude to arrange their laws in such fashion as the greatest number suppose to make for their greatest happiness. This may be done with tardy clumsiness, or with that hastier clumsiness which we term Revolution. But the obstacles to this process in civilised countries are no longer picturesque; and the poet, though not yet the statesman, has already to face that difficulty which John Stuart Mill felt in the background.   When we have rectified all the anomalies which the Radical Reformer—not yet the Socialist— can discover, what are we to turn to next? For that perplexity, as he has told us, Mill found a solution which met the needs of his individual soul.   It lay in the study of the poems of Wordsworth.   But although this was in fact (as I shall later try to show) the best line of thought open to that philosopher, there is here no hint of fresh general occupation for the human race as a whole.   Rather it suggests to us, what the subsequent history of thought has confirmed, that we are now thrown back upon fundamental problems ; that before the race can make out for itself a new practical ideal—such as Plenty and Liberty were once to the many, and such as Science is now to the few—we must somehow achieve a profound readjustment of our general views of the mean-ing of life and of the structure of the universe.

And, in fact, with this great upheaval of thought Mr. Swinburne, by the mere force of circumstances, finds himself largely concerned. It is not that his main interest is in philo-

sophical speculation ; his main interest is in
literature and poetry. But he has the intelligence to catch, the voice to utter, whatever
speculation is in the air around him ; and
assuredly some of the utterances to which his
receptive but, so to say, detached and disinterested genius prompts him, surpass Lucretius
himself in the singularity of their divergence
from the traditional stream of human thought
and song.

We are bound to face the possibility that the
human race came into existence from the operation of purely physical causes, and that there
may therefore be in all the universe no beings
higher than ourselves ; not even the remote and
indifferent gods of the Lucretian heaven. By
many modern minds, in whom the sense of pity
for unmerited suffering and the desire for ideal
justice have become passionately strong, this
conception, which absolutely negatives the
possibility of any pity or justice more efficacious
than our own, is felt as an abiding nightmare,
which seems from time to time to deepen into
a terrible reality. This is the mood of mind
illustrated in its extreme form in Tennyson's
" Despair." Yet this very hypothesis has inspired

one of Mr. Swinburne's most exultant poems,
the magnificent " Hymn of Man," too well known
to need more than a few lines of quotation :—

> In the gray beginning of years, in the twilight of
>   things that began,
> The word of the earth in the ears of the world, was
>   it God ? was it man ? . . .
> When her eyes new-born of the night saw yet no star
>   out of reach ;
> When her maiden mouth was alight with the flame of
>   musical speech ;
> When her virgin feet were set on the terrible heavenly
>   way,
> And her virginal lids were wet with the dew of the
>   birth of the day ; . . .
> Did her heart rejoice, and the might of her spirit
>   exult in her then,
> Child, yet no child of the night, and motherless
>   mother of men ?

Æneadum genetrix, so sang Lucretius in the
same tone long ago, personifying, with a half-
ironical enthusiasm, the blind Power which ruled
his world ; which had no care for human virtue
or human pain :—

> Nec bene promeritis capitur, nec tangitur ira.

Still more striking is the long passage in
which Tristram of Lyonesse proudly avows,

before the great spectacle of the universe, the inevitable nothingness of man.

Ay, what of these ? but, O strong sun ! O sea !
I bid not you, divine things ! comfort me,
I stand not up to match you in your sight ;
Who hath said ye have mercy toward us, ye who
    have might ? . . .
For if in life or death be aught of trust,
And if some unseen just God or unjust
Put soul into the body of natural things,
And in Time's pauseless feet and world-wide wings
Some spirit of impulse and some sense of will,
That steers them thro' the seas of good and ill,
To some incognisable and actual end,
Be it just or unjust, foe to man or friend,
How should we make the stable spirit to swerve,
How teach the strong soul of the world to serve, . . .
The streams flow back toward whence the springs
    began,
That less of thirst might sear the lips of man ?

Mr. Swinburne, of course, knows as well as anybody what answer man, in all his insignificance, makes to such appeals as these. When Tristram asks :—

Hath he such eyes as, when the shadows flee,
The sun looks out with to salute the sea ?

we answer ; Nay ; but he has eyes that can weep ; and therefore in a moral universe no

" great blazing lump," be it sun or Sirius, could
be of so much account as he.

But in these poems at any rate we have the
most striking extant record of an important
phase of thought.   We have the strict materialistic synthesis clad in its most splendid colouring, and its most inexorable scorn of men.

Growing out of this there is another phase
of thought which also Mr. Swinburne has presented with singular fire.   That is the resolve
that even if there be no moral purpose already
in the world, man shall put it there ; that even
if all evolution be necessarily truncated, yet
moral evolution, so long as our race lasts, there
shall be ; that even if man's virtue be momentary, he shall act as though it were an eternal
gain.   This noble theme inspires the verses
called " The Pilgrims," too familiar for long
quotation here :—

—Is this so sweet that one were fain to follow?
Is this so sure where all men's hopes are hollow,
        Even this your dream, that by much tribulation
        Ye shall make whole flawed hearts and bowed
                necks straight?
—Nay, though our life were blind, our death were
                fruitless,
Not therefore were the whole world's high hope
        rootless ;

But man to man, nation would turn to nation,
And the old life live, and the old great word
   be great.

Fine as this is, there is a vagueness about
the offered promise which leaves the wisdom of
the Pilgrims' self-sacrifice open to more than
one criticism.   For, on the one hand, Science
looks coldly on the notion of interfering with
our present well-being for the advantage of
distant generations—preferring to remind us
that we know so little of the conditions of life
even a hundred years hence that, with the best
intentions, it would be no easy matter to
benefit any one more remote than our grand-
children ; and, on the other hand, the gentle
cynical philosophy which spoke through the
mouth of M. Renan bids us note that, inasmuch
as man's whole existence may very possibly be
the *mauvaise plaisanterie* of some irresponsible
Power, it will be judicious so to act as to be
able at the worst to assure ourselves that we
have never been completely taken in.

Whatever, indeed, of wisdom rather than of
cynicism this advice contains has been ex-
emplified by Mr. Swinburne's career ; for he
has given himself whole-heartedly to an object

which is neither selfish nor unworthy, and yet
which is in some sense independent of what
the universe may be or do.   I need not say
that I mean the Art of Poetry ; which for
himself forms an adequate issue from these
deeper perplexities, although it is ill adapted
for mankind at large, since it absolutely requires
the possession of genius.   A world of amateur
art is not in itself an ideal.

Poetic imagination leads Mr. Swinburne, as
is natural, to the expression of various other
moods of mind, not necessarily consistent with
the mood of " The Pilgrims."   Thus the
Lucretian satisfaction at liberation from the
terrors of religion forms the theme of a beautiful roundel :—

We have drunken of Lethe at last, we have eaten of
    lotus ;
  What hurts it us here that sorrows are born and
    die ?
We have said to the dream that caressed and the
    dread that smote us,
      Good-night and good-bye.

Or sometimes he dwells simply upon the
fact that we die, and that our loves perish with
us ; but dwells on it somehow as with an intelligence interested in noting that fact, rather

than with a heart that feels it as inmost
pain.

Or they loved their life through, and then went
    whither ?
  And were one to the end—but what end who
    knows ?
Love deep as the sea as a rose must wither,
  As the rose-red seaweed that mocks the rose.
Shall the dead take thought for the dead to love
    them ?
  What love was ever as deep as a grave ?
They are loveless now as the grass above them,
      Or the wave.

I know not what in the easy brilliancy of
these lines gives the impression that they are
an imaginative description of the inhabitants of
some other planet, or at least that Thalassius is
as much concerned for his sea-weed as for anything else. And of all Swinburne's poems,
perhaps the most wonderful, with melody
farthest beyond the reach of any other still
living man, is that " Garden of Proserpine,"
whose close represents in well-known words
the deep life-weariness of men who have had
enough of love. There is here far more than
the Lucretian satisfaction in the thought that
we shall sleep tranquilly through the hazardous
future as we slept tranquilly through the raging

past—*ad confligendum venientibus undique Pœnis*
—when all the perils which menaced Rome
were as nothing to us yet unborn.   No, there
is here a profounder renouncement of life ;
there is the grim suspicion which has stolen
into many a heart, that we do in truth feel
within us, as years go by, a mortality of spirit
as well as flesh ; that the " bower of unimagined
flower and tree " withers inevitably into a frozen
barrenness from which no new life can
spring :—

> And love, grown faint and fretful,
> With lips but half regretful
> Sighs, and with eyes forgetful
>   Weeps that no loves endure.

When we turn from Swinburne to William
Morris we pass into a very different emotional
clime.   Similar as the two poets are in
thoroughness of artistic culture and in width of
learning, the personal temperaments which their
poems reveal are in some sense complementary.
In Swinburne we have seen the vivid but detached intelligence rendering in turn with equal
eloquence, and apparently with equal satisfaction, every attitude of mind which the known
cosmic laws, construed strictly as against man's

hopes, can be shown to justify. In Morris we
have a man equally hopeless indeed, but not
equally indifferent to hope—steeped, rather, in
all the delicate joys, the soft emotions, which
make the charm of life, and feeling at every
turn with sad discouragement the shadow and
imminence of the End.   He is above all things
the poet of Love ; but in his poems love is
never without the note of yearning, the sense
of an unseizable and fugitive joy :—

Love is enough : while ye deemed him a-sleeping,
    There were signs of his coming and sounds of
        his feet ;
His touch it was that would bring you to weeping,
    When the summer was deepest and music most
        sweet ;
    In his footsteps ye followed the day to its dying,
Ye went forth by his gown-skirts the morning to
        meet :
    In his place on the beaten-down orchard-grass
        lying,
    Of the sweet ways ye pondered yet left for life's
        trying.

We   asked   ourselves   but   now   whether
Liberty, which Swinburne sang, could still be
said to offer a permanent motive and object in
life for the mass of mankind.   To this question
Morris has an unexpectedly definite answer.

He desires, indeed, a reconstruction of society far more radical than the mere republican demands. He embarks with light heart on a task which one might have thought difficult enough to supply the world with unrealised ideals for a thousand years. Yet he believes that this socialistic reconstruction will be effected so rapidly that the problem as to the subsequent aims and occupations of mankind confronts us almost at once. And, as the stanza above quoted suggests, it is in Love that he finds the main, though not the only, interest of the happy and equalised race to be.

Now we may certainly say that just as Liberty represents the next stage of human progress after Peace and Plenty, so does Love represent the next stage beyond Liberty. When men have got their communities arranged to their mind, they will find time—as a number of leisured persons find time already—to devote their main attention to such happiness as the relation between the sexes can bring. But here, almost for the first time, the question of the unknown future begins to have a practical bearing on life. If love is at once brought thus into prominence and also deprived of all beyond its earthly fruition, is there not a fear lest it should either sink into mere animal passion or lose its tranquillity in yearning pain? Morris has treated this question in two ways; answering it generally in the sadder tone, and as though from actual experience; but once with resolute cheerfulness, in a polemical composition. Let us take this latter first.

It is sometimes urged as an advantage attending the loss of belief in a future life that those who count this life as all are more eager to make their fellow-men happy in it. Without further assenting to this view, we may admit that Morris's belief in earth as the only possible Paradise has helped to drive him, by the most generous road, into a socialism where we may watch him tossing between various Scyllæ and Charybdes with which we are not here concerned. What now interests us is the delightful romance in which he has described earthly life led happily, with no thought of life beyond. What to retain, what to relinquish, has here been carefully thought out. Religion and philosophy disappear altogether; science and poetry are in the background; but we are left with the decorative arts, open-air exercise, and an

abundance of beautiful and innocent girls.   The
future of the human race, in short, is to be a
kind of affectionate picnic.

I know not, indeed, how the given problem
could have been more attractively solved.   But
how long will life last thus, à la Rousseau ?
Will the haymaking lovers go on haymaking
for countless generations and still keep their
emotions at precisely the right temperature ?
Dangers of one kind need no insistence ; and
as for troubles in a higher air, it may be noted
that nothing in " News from Nowhere " strikes a
truer note than the author's yearning regret at
severance from his bewitching heroine — the
daughter of a world to be.   He feels that in
order to live her life he must himself be
changed ; and although he speaks of the needed
change as if it were but a forgetting of pain and
sorrow, a re-entry into Eden, — yet when we
compare his picture of that ideal life with his or
any active man's life here and now, we feel that
there will be more loss than gain ; and that the
fuller pleasure cannot compensate for the absence
of moral evolution.

That old and just gravamen against almost
all theological paradises — that they provide for

joy but not for progress—holds good of Morris's many imagined paradises as well. They are abodes of unchanging bliss, dimly felt to be in themselves unsatisfactory, though attractive in comparison with the briefer pleasures which man's common life affords. If they are to be enjoyed without satiety, there must, as in " Ogier the Dane," be a transformation of personality, a forgetfulness of the heroic deeds and strenuous joys of earth. Yet, on the other hand, these strenuous joys are never felt to have any clear advantage over the amorous paradises, on account of their hazardous shortness. Orpheus gains no victory in argument over the Sirens, whose invitations would be irresistible if there were not so much reason to suspect their good faith. And in the " Hill of Venus," that most terrible of all pictures of remorseful satiety, a Christian hope has to be invoked in order that there may seem to be any other alternative than endless loathing or endless death.

Perhaps, indeed, the fact may be that man is not constructed for flawless happiness, but for moral evolution. Few passages in Morris are more affecting than those in which the Wanderers, who have failed to find the Acre of

the Undying, express at once their half-shame
at having undertaken that quest, and their regret
that it has been all in vain.   In the lines in
which their poet pleads their excuse, he manages
to remind the reader of many valid reasons
which impel to that bootless desire :—

> Ah, doubt and fear they well might have indeed.
> Cry out upon them, ye who have no need
> Of life, to right the blindness and the wrong !
> Think scorn of these, ye who are made so strong
> That with no good-night ye can loose the hand
> That led you erst thro' Love's sweet flowery land !
> Laugh, ye whose eyes are piercing to behold
> What makes the silver seas and skies of gold !
> Pass by in haste, ye folk, who day by day
> Win all desires that lie upon your way !

It is from no lack of sympathy with heroism
that Morris has tarried in this world of soft
regrets.   Seldom have heroic passion, god-like
endeavour, been so painted as in that scene
between Sigurd and Brynhild on the summit of
Hind-fell :—

And where on the wings of his hope is the spirit of
    Sigurd borne ?

But all that triumphant adventure rests in the
last resort on the existence of Odin and his
halls of gold ; Odin, seen sometimes in visible

form, and encouraging the younger heroes with
memory of their sires, whose valour reaps now
its high reward :—

For on earth they thought of my threshold, and the
    gifts I have to give,
Nor prayed for a little longer, and a little longer to
    live.

It is the privilege of poetry thus "simple,
sensuous, and passionate" that the singer can
reveal himself without self-consciousness, and
utter without loss of dignity the inward softness
of the strong. Who has dwelt longer than this
robust and manly worker in that sunlit mist of
yearning which hangs suspended above the
watershed of joy and pain ? Who has breathed
more intimately the last forlornness, and such
an inward cry as oftenest is only guessed in a
tear ?

Come down, O love, may not our hands still meet,
Since still we live to-day, forgetting June,
Forgetting May, deeming October sweet—
—O hearken, hearken ! through the afternoon,
The gray tower sings a strange old tinkling tune !
Sweet, sweet and sad, the failing year's last breath,
Too satiate of life to strive with death.

And we too—will it not be soft and kind,
That rest from life, from patience and from pain,

That rest from bliss we know not when we find,
That rest from Love which ne'er the end can gain ?—
—Hark, how the tune swells, that erewhile did wane !
Look up, love ! ah, cling close and never move !
How can I have enough of life and love ?

If in these October stanzas we have the last fruitless attempt at resignation, in the poem which preludes to November we have a mood more dreadful still. We have the recognition that the Cosmos has no true place for man ; we have that underlying aspect of Nature which, once seized, is no less than appalling ; when the familiar garden seems alien and terrible as a gulf in the Milky Way ; and, nakedly confronted with the everlasting universe, man that must die feels more than the bitterness of death,

> Look out upon the real world, where the moon,
> Half-way 'twixt root and crown of these high trees,
> Turns the dead midnight into dreamy noon,
> Silent and full of wonders, for the breeze
> Died at the sunset, and no images,
> No hopes of day, are left in sky or earth ;—
> Is it not fair, and of most wondrous worth ?
>
> Yea, I have looked and seen November there ;
> The changeless seal of change it seemed to be,
> Fair death of things that, living once, were fair,
> Bright sign of loneliness too great for me,'

Strange image of the dread eternity,
In whose void patience how can these have part,
These outstretched feverish hands, this restless
    heart ?

We have traced in the work of these two
poets almost every mood of feeling possible to
high-minded men under the shadow of an inevitable doom.   There has been courage, and
there has been calm ; there has been the solemn
sadness of impossible resignation, and that
imperious cry for Life ! more Life ! which is the
very voice of the human heart.   Is this then
all ? and must poets in every age be content to
renew the old desiring, and to fall back baffled
from the same impalpable wall of gloom ?

There are still those among us who will
answer, Nay.   There are still those who, while
accepting to the full the methods and the results
of Science, will .not yet surrender the ancient
hopes of our race.   And we shall point out
that these poets, while strictly within their
rights in assuming nothing which Science has
not sanctioned, have yet omitted from their
purview no trifling part of human thought,
belief, and emotion.   They have taken no heed
of the traditions, the instincts, the phenomena

which have led men to believe in another world
mixed with ours.   They have ignored what the
still greater poet to whom we now come has
called

> the silent Word
> Of that world-prophet in the heart of man.

We shall not let our case go thus by
default.   We shall urge that although the
cosmic laws now known are *neutral*—for that
they are *adverse* we certainly shall not admit
—it is most certain that there are still cosmic
laws unknown, and that of these there may
well be some one within range of discovery
which may govern more directly the region in
which these problems lie.   We shall do well,
therefore, to consider whether there be any
primary belief held in common by all religions ;
and, if so, whether that belief is capable of
being expressed in a form in which it might
conceivably be proved by Science to be a
cosmical law—a fourth law lying at the root of
Psychology as those other laws at the root of
Physics and Biology.   If we can do this we
shall at least know where we are and what we
have to aim at ; and the controversy, which
is now too often like a fight between a dog and

a fish,—between the subjective instincts which glide in the ocean and the objective facts which bark on the shore,—may be conducted in something more resembling a common element.

It is plain that the thesis upon which we are to combine must in some way express our belief in a spiritual world. But it will not be enough to affirm the *co-existence* of such a world with our own ; for mere co-existence will be incapable of proof. Nor, on the other hand, must we call upon mankind to believe that the two worlds are in reality *one*, or that the material world is shadow and illusion, and the spiritual world real alone. This, again, is a dogma beyond the possible reach of experiment. Let us take a middle term, and speak of the *interaction* or *interpenetration* of the two worlds. If we believe that a spiritual world has in any way been manifested to mankind, we must suppose that mankind has in some way been perceptible to that world as well. There will therefore have been *interaction* between the two. Or the word *interpenetration* will include both nay manifest interaction, and also those vaguer intimations " of something far more deeply interfused " which we cannot afford to despise,

although we must not put them forward as
evidence for a possibly demonstrable cosmic
law.

It is on the ground, then, of their association
with this assumed fourth cosmic law of interpenetrating worlds that I would claim both for
Wordsworth and for Tennyson a commanding
place among the teachers of this century. I do
not, of course, claim a *scientific* eminence for
poets, one of whom was ignorantly hostile to
Science, while the other, although neither hostile
nor ignorant, wrote no memoirs and made no
experiments. But certain truths ultimately
provable by science may be in the first instance
attained by other than scientific methods.
They may rise into consciousness, as I have
elsewhere tried to show,[1] in some sense ready-
made, and accompanied with no logical perception of the processes which, deep in our being,
may have been used to reach them. The
"genius" shown in discovery or in creative art
may be defined as "an uprush of subliminal
faculty," and the rapt absorption of a Newton,
the waking dream of a Raphael, the inward

[1] " The Mechanism of Genius," *Proceedings of the Society for
Psychical Research* (Trübner), Part xxii.

audition of a Mozart, do but represent the same process occurring in different regions of thought and emotion. The mystic claims a like inspiration; but since we have no canons by which to test the validity of the message which he brings us, we do well for the most part to set mystic messages aside altogether. But nevertheless just as Faraday, by making many provably true divinations in the physical universe, secured mankind's attention for certain divinations which he could not prove ; so also may a great poet, by manifestly fruitful inspirations in his own special art, claim our attention for alleged inspirations in a field where our critical tests can no longer follow him. The fact that fools have rushed in is not in itself a reason for angels to fear to tread. High art is based upon unprovable intuitions ; and of all arts it is Poetry whose intuitions take the brightest glow, and best illumine the mystery without us from the mystery within.

Few poets, indeed, in any age have thus deserved the name of prophet ; to fewer still ought we to grant it in such an age as our own. For we shall need to be assured that the prophet's convictions come neither from tradi-

tion nor from temperament ; that he is not
buoyed up by mere personal gladness, nor
heedless of the austere rejoinders which Science
has made to many a facile hope.   It is well that
Tennyson should have shown at every stage his
readiness for stern self-questioning, for the fac-
ing of naked truth : it is well that the " empy-
real heights of thought " of *In Memoriam*, xciv.,
should have been followed by the grim alternatives of cxix.——" I trust I have not wasted
breath " ;——that the mystical glory of " The
Voice and the Peak " should have left him still
capable of shuddering with the nightmare of
a godless world in his incomparable " Despair."
For thus we discern him as a spirit which has
scaled from abyss to summit the whole ascen-
sion open to incarnate man ; one who from
deep discouragement, from melancholy isolation,
has slowly climbed the " Mount of Vision,"
and has uttered thence his auguries, meet for
the wise to hear.

Well also that, like his own Akbar promulgating " the Divine Faith," he has infused the
least possible of the special or the transitory into
his appeal for eternal things.   For it is in very
truth the *desiderium orbis catholici* which our

prophet's voice must meet ; with some such
authoritative inauguration and prophetic herald-
ing as has ushered in each great successive expansion of the conceptions and ideals of men.

I know not how soon Science may sanction
the prophet's hope ;—Science which after her
first flush of all-conquering achievement begins
to realise anew that " A thousand things are
hidden still, And not a hundred known." But
in an epoch of transition and bewilderment
great souls make the surest harbourage ; and
even as for the storm-tost philosopher early in
this century the best haven lay in the poems of
Wordsworth, so now in the poems of Tennyson
lies the best haven for men far more numerous
and in far worse straits, at our troubled century's
close.

I have placed Wordsworth and Tennyson
together as realising with extraordinary intuition,
promulgating with commanding genius, the
interpenetration of the spiritual and the material
worlds.   But between Wordsworth's poems and
the more significant of Tennyson's, Darwin had
given " the holding turn " to man's growing belief in the Law of Evolution.   And it was the
influence, however indirect, of this *third* law of

the Cosmos which enabled the later Laureate to enrich and deepen his predecessor's conception of the *fourth*.   To Wordsworth the sense of the soul in Nature was in itself an all-sufficing joy. He felt it, and he was at peace.   But with Tennyson the fourth law at once completes the third, and is confirmed by it.   For with the affirmation of a spiritual universe he links a claim for moral evolution.

The one conception, of course, does not necessarily imply the other.   If worlds inter-penetrate they do not interpenetrate for the special benefit of man.   Their interaction must be a great structural fact in the Cosmos, a fundamental reality reaching backward through-out an immeasurable past.   Existing before man was thought of, it may exist now with no thought for man.

But, on the other hand, here we have a new possibility which alone will explain the perturba-tions and complete the lacunæ of the older generalisation.   If man is now interacting with a spiritual world, he may act and advance in that world, for aught we know, for ever ; and in that case Evolution may be no longer a partial and truncated, but a universal and endless law.

" What hurts it us here if planets are born and die ? "   What need we care for the shrinking sun, the squandered energy, the omen of the moon's frozen peace ?   If man's soul grow for ever, it matters no more how many solar systems she wears out than how many coats.

Nevertheless, to correspond with this expansion without us, there must be an expansion within.   If man is to march with the Cosmos, it must be progress and not joy which is his goal.   Thus alone can we rally to the standard of Life all that is bravest and most generous, as well as all that is most native and ineradicable in the human heart.

Glory of warrior, glory of orator, glory of song,
 Paid with a voice flying by to be lost on an endless
  sea—
Glory of Virtue, to fight, to struggle, to right the
  wrong—
 Nay, but she aim'd not at glory, no lover of glory
  she :
Give her the glory of going on, and still to be.

The wages of sin is death : if the wages of Virtue be
  dust,
 Would she have heart to endure for the life of the
  worm and the fly ?
She desires no isles of the blest, no quiet seats of the
  just,

> To rest in a golden grove, or to bask in a summer
>   sky :
> Give her the wages of going on, and not to die.

Σάλπιγξ δ' ἀϋτῆ πάντ' ἐκεῖν' ἐπέφλεγεν. This
cry is the trumpet-call of man's true salvation ;
the summons to no houri-haunted paradise,
no passionless contemplation, no monotony of
prayer and praise ; but to endless advance by
endless effort, and, if need be, by endless pain.
Still shall be asked, amid vaster alternatives, the
stern question of Cato :—

> utrumne secundis
> An magis adversis staret Romana propago ?

Still shall cause produce effect ; still shall all
that is be transmuted and not destroyed.   Let
no man trust to an instant deliverance, nor dream
of an age-long peace.   For thus our modern
thought has risen at last to the height of the
solitary Plotinus ; who, when he was told that
the shade of Hercules in the meadow of asphodel
rejoiced in the great deeds that he had done,
replied that the shade of Hercules might boast
thus to shades ; but that the true Hercules
accounted all past deeds as nought, " being
transported   into   a   more   sacred   place,   and

strenuously engaging, even above his strength,
in those contests in which the wise engage."

Is not this, at last and undoubtedly, the true
hope and ideal of man ?   Is not all well, if to
this end the cosmic laws be working, and Fate's
tangled web be spun ?   Prospects vast as these
cannot be provable, nay, cannot be truly defin-
able nor clearly imaginable by man.   But that
which for us is the vital point,—the actual fact
of the interaction of material and spiritual
worlds,—this surely, as I have already hinted,
ought to be ultimately capable of demonstration.
The human end to the chain can at least be
investigated, the human sensitivity tested, the
human testimony weighed.   On this topic I
shall not here dwell at length.   It may suffice
to say that there are those who, however
imperfectly, are endeavouring to perform this
plain duty ; and that to these men Lord Tennyson, almost from the inception of their task, gave
the support of his name.   Neither shall I
attempt to assemble the passages, some of them
quoted in the preceding essay, from which the
grounds of this sympathy may be more or less
plainly inferred.   But I will remind the reader
that for any estimation of Tennyson's final

opinions, the later poems are, of course, the most
significant.   In his last years there was inequality of poetic merit,—an inequality which
admitted nevertheless of more than one master-
piece ; but there was no decline in intellectual
grasp and power.   Nay, I think that all will
some day recognise that there was even a lifelong
gain in wisdom ; a lifelong maintenance of that
position, in sympathy with and yet in advance
of his time, which was first manifest when *In
Memoriam*—now so intelligible and so orthodox
—perplexed as well as charmed the reading
public of its earlier day.

From " The Ancient Sage," which (with the
fully concordant " Akbar's Dream ") approaches
perhaps as nearly as any of the poet's works to
a personal creed or testament, comes the passage
which I have prefixed as motto to this essay ;
and also this other passage, treating of the
possible development of powers as yet un-
recognised in man :—

My son, the world is dark with griefs and graves,
So dark that men cry out against the Heavens.
Who knows but that the darkness is in man ?
The doors of Night may be the gates of Light ;
For wert thou born or blind or deaf, and then
Suddenly heal'd, how would'st thou glory in all

The splendours and the voices of the world !
And we, the poor earth's dying race, and yet
No phantoms, watching from a phantom shore
Await the last and largest sense to make
The phantom walls of this illusion fade,
And show us that the world is wholly fair.

The volumes called *Demeter and other Poems*,
and *The Death of Œnone*, published since my
former essay, contain some very definite indications of the poet's later views. We must remember
that it was his habit to scatter pregnant sayings
in unexpected places ; and that his sincerity
and scrupulosity of style allow us to dwell with
confidence on his briefest expressions. Compare,
then, with a well-known passage in " Aylmer's
Field " these lines from " Demeter " :—

Last as the likeness of a dying man,
Without his knowledge, from him flits to warn
A far-off friendship that he comes no more.

And observe, in " Happy," the poet's anticipation
of the full evolution of this faculty of direct
communication in the spiritual world :—

When we shall stand transfigured, like Christ on
Hermon hill,
And moving each to music, soul in soul and light in
light,
Shall flash thro' one another in a moment as we
will.

Consider, too, all that is implied in the following
passage from " The Ring "; a poem quasi-
dramatic in form, but in which the principal
speaker, apart from the actual story, seems a
mere vehicle for reflections not obviously other
than Tennyson's own :—

> The Ghost in Man, the Ghost that once was Man,
> But cannot wholly free itself from Man,
> Are calling to each other thro' a dawn
> Stranger than earth has ever seen ; the veil
> Is rending, and the Voices of the day
> Are heard across the Voices of the dark.
> No sudden heaven, nor sudden hell, for man,
> But thro' the Will of One who knows and rules—
> And utter knowledge is but utter love—
> Æonian Evolution, swift or slow,
> Thro' all the Spheres—an ever opening height,
> An ever lessening earth.

The conception of endless progress with
which this passage concludes is resumed in a
form characteristic enough of the bard's personality in the lines " By an Evolutionist ":—

> The Lord let the house of a brute to the soul of a
>   man,
>   And the man said " Am I your debtor ? "
> And the Lord—" Not yet : but make it as clean as
>   you can,
>   And then I will let you a better."

.   .   .   .

I have climb'd to the snows of Age, and I gaze at a
    field in the Past,
    Where I sank with the body at times in the sloughs
        of a low desire,
But I hear no yelp of the beast, and the Man is quiet
    at last
    As he stands on the heights of his life with a
        glimpse of a height that is higher.

Here surely is the answer to that despair of
man's moral vitality which "weeps that no
loves endure"; to that *gran rifiuto* of Life and
Progress which craves only "the sleep eternal
in an eternal night." "Eld and Death" have
not hushed at least this song; but from the
great old age of this grave and meditative man
his trumpet-call sounds ever more solemnly
triumphant; and Death, whose "truer name is
Onward," is discerned auspicious and anear.
The lesson of Evolution, as this Evolutionist
delivers it to us, is "Lay hold on Life! For
Life the Universe is making; help thou that
Life to be!" The final purpose, indeed, which
we may thus subserve, lies far beyond the grasp
of men. But while we still subserve it—through
stress, perchance, and strenuous pain—how
easily may those ancient longings of the human
spirit find their fulfilment by the way! That

joy of the poet in Nature, that exultation in the stormy or shining universe : where is its limit now ? And as for the heart's deeper needs, all that the " idle singer " sang in our empty day ; —shall not the lovers learn, in Plato's words, " what it was that they had so long been desir- ing," and perceive why through earth's close caresses those loved ones seemed still so far, and their impalpable tokens of amity were more thrilling than any cruder joy? Shall they not recognise that no terrene Matter or Energy, but Love itself is the imperishable of that higher world ; so that earth's brief encounter with some spirit, quickly dear, may be the precursory omen of a far-off espousal, or the unconscious recognition of fond long-severed souls ? Shall they not find that the lifelong loyalty to the touch of a vanished hand has been no vain or one-sided offering of the heart ; but that the affection has been stablished by an unseen companionship, and that the Beloved has answered all ? *Id cinerem et Manis credo curare sepultos.*

And what of " the Nameless of the hundred names " ? Does our conception of infinite interpenetration, infinite evolution, infinite unity,

raise us to clearer vision of that "whole world-
self and all-in-all"?

The sun, the moon, the stars, the seas, the hills and
    the plains—
Are not these, O Soul, the Vision of Him who reigns?

Speak to Him thou for He hears, and Spirit with
    Spirit can meet—
Closer is He than breathing, and nearer than hands
    and feet.

And the ear of man cannot hear, and the eye of man
    cannot see;
But if we could see and hear, this Vision—were it
    not He?

In every age the Poet has looked round him
on the universe, and spokesmen of our race have
set down in solemn language the impress left
upon the soul.   First of all come Homer's lines,
majestic, unsurpassable ; forging the very art of
poetry with the same Titan strokes as Achilles'
shield :—

  Ἐν μὲν γαῖαν ἔτευξ', ἐν δ' οὐρανὸν, ἐν δὲ θάλασσαν,
  Ἠελιόντ' ἀκάμαντα σελήνην τε πλήθουσαν—

But these lines and those that follow have no
philosophy behind them.   They are a naked
triumphant inventory of "the whole world and
creatures of God."

And then, as the Ionian youth begins to decline into questioning sadness, we have that catalogue of the disenchanted Menander—Menander, who held that man most blest of all,

῞Οστις θεωρήσας ἀλύπως, Παρμένων,
Τὰ σεμνὰ ταῦτ', ἀπῆλθεν, ὅθεν ἦλθεν, ταχύ—

who having looked once upon those glorious objects, this spectacle of sun and night and sea, should then pass satisfied and swiftly from a life which had nought else so reverend to show.

And next comes Virgil's monumental enumeration :—

Principio cælum ac terras camposque liquentis,
Lucentemque globum Lunæ, Titaniaque astra,—

and those succeeding lines which have become the Roman charter of a spiritual world, the epigraph writ across the heavens to testify that there is a Mind in the universe, a Soul within the sum of things. And, lastly, we have Tennyson penetrating to a still profounder identification ; to the sense that what we have held far off and future, that verily is here and now ; and that what is in truth the Nameless, that is our world and we ; " for we here are in God's bosom, a land unknown."

P

All men mourn the poet.   But those of us who cling to the spiritual aspect of the universe have more than a great poet to mourn.   We have lost our head and our chief ; the one man, surely, in all the world to-day, who from a towering eminence which none could question affirmed the realities which to us are all.   For him we may repeat Lucretius' homage to the sage and poet whom that other island " bore within her three-cornered shores " ;—that Sicily,

Quæ cum magna modis multis miranda videtur
Gentibus humanis regio, visendaque fertur,
Rebus opima bonis, multa munita virum vi,—
Nil tamen hoc habuisse viro præclarius in se,
Nec sanctum magis et mirum carumque videtur.

Our island too " in many ways is marvellous, and such as folk come far to see ; laden she is with riches and guarded with great force of men ; yet seems she to have held within her borders nothing than this man more glorious, nothing more holy, wonderful, and dear."

LEOPOLD, DUKE OF ALBANY :—IN MEMORIAM

[Written as a private memoir, and published (1884) by desire.]

'Αλλά με σός τε πόθος σά τε μήδεα, φαίδιμ' 'Οδυσσεῦ,
Σή τ' ἀγανοφροσύνη μελιηδέα θυμὸν ἀπηύρα.

To those who love to watch the shaping of
character, that subtle intertexture of ancestral
and individual warp and woof, there is always
something interesting, almost pathetic, in the
sight of a young life which springs up amid
fixed hereditary surroundings, and has to accom-
modate its fresh impulses to the strong tradition
of bygone men.   From the legend of Buddha
downwards, there has been many a royal
romance in which the interest has turned on
the young spirit's self-liberation from the tram-
melling conditions, its resolute emergence into
a freer and higher life.   But there are other

cases, not less worth record, where the progress
of the inward drama has led, not to the casting
off of hereditary usages or duties, but to their
voluntary and fruitful acceptance, to the gradual
self-identification of the new life with the old—
the absorption of personal ambitions or pleasures
in the *mos majorum*, the ancient vocation of
the race.

In the case of an English Prince there can
be no doubt in which of these directions an
upward progress must tend.   There can be no
summons from without which leads to higher
serviceableness than that great birthright duly
used ; a young life needs no better aim than
to become such that the English people may
account it as truly royal.   And it was in this
process of widening conceptions, of quickening
conscience, that the great interest of Prince
Leopold's career consisted for those who
watched him with anxiously loving eyes.   His
inward drama lay in the gradual transformation
of his boyish idea of royal descent as a title to
enjoyment, hampered by wearisome restraints,
to his manlier view of that high birth as a
summons to duty, and his willing submission
to its accompanying restrictions, as part and

parcel of the calling which his whole heart
embraced.

It is at Windsor Castle, when he was fifteen
years old, that these recollections begin. He was
then a most engaging boy ; with the physical
charm which accompanies the union of high
spirit with fragile delicacy, and the moral charm
of a nature whose affections, at once vivid and
diffident, seemed to beseech the regard and
notice which all who knew him were eager to
bestow. He had already attracted the earnest
good-will, the serious hopes of many of the
leading men of the time, and already in his
autograph book was conspicuous that maxim,
from Archbishop Trench's hand, which should
be written on all tablets and engraved on all
hearts of princes—

> O righteous doom, that they who make
>   Pleasure their only end,
> Ordering the whole life for its sake,
>   Miss that whereto they tend.
>
> But they who bid stern Duty lead,
>   Content to follow, they
> Of Duty only taking heed,
>   Find pleasure by the way.

The impetuous boy had not yet risen to

any such level as this.   He was at an age when
the desire for companionship, action, adventure,
begins to be strong ; and the glimpses which
his Etonian visitors gave him of a free world of
games and friendships formed a tantalising
contrast to his carefully guarded days.   This
impulse, this disappointment, were to last
throughout his life.   His strong innate tendency
towards active amusements—riding, dancing,
social gaieties of all kinds—was destined always
to urge him to efforts beyond his strength.   And
now in boyhood, with health even more delicate than in adult years, he had many hours of
restless indolence, of idle beating against the
bars of his fate.   And indeed to one who has
not yet the force for independent action or
pleasure, the life of Windsor Castle must sometimes seem as if it were conceived on too vast
a scale, and established too immutably, for the
needs of a young and ardent spirit.   The tramp
of the sentinel beneath the windows, the martial
music at dawn of day, even the stately sym-
metry of the avenues which radiate from the
Central Keep—all signs of pomp are signs also
of circumscription, and the concrete embodiment
of eight hundred years of monarchy weighs

heavily on the individual heart. The pacings
of a vague unrest have sounded along many a
terrace fringed with flowers, in Home Park, and
Hollow Garden, and Orangery, and on the
steep Slopes of the royal hill.

But all this must needs be so ; and human life
itself might seem to lose in dignity were there not
something of solemn and symbolical in the ordering of earth's greatest home.   In any training for
the summits either of hereditary position or of
individual genius the danger in our time is from
relaxation rather than from restraint. The young
tree must not branch too soon ; its sap must rise
in steady spiral if it is to reach a height—

> Ubi aera vincere summum
> Arboris haud ullæ jactu potuere sagittæ.

And at Windsor there was much more than
state ; there were the family affections, made
more unique by isolation ;—the maternal
solicitude which, from the first to the last day
of that son's life, no cares of State could ever
distract or slacken ;—the companionship both
of the younger and of that just-elder sister
whose romantic girlhood lavished its wealth of
love on him.   And there was much of the

buoyancy as well as of the restlessness of early
youth ; there were happy wanderings amid the
boskages of the park, where the Angora goats
which he loved to watch flecked the foreground
with their soft whiteness, and the Castle's
bastions closed the vista with wall of steadfast gray.   And indoors, too, were merry
mockeries and bursts of boyish sportiveness,
racings along the endless passages, hidings in
the niches of ancient walls, climbings to the
Round Tower's roof, beneath the Flag of
England, in the rushing sunny air.

The first time, perhaps, when he seemed to
awake to a sense of his own part in historic
greatness was when the Garter had just been
bestowed on him, in April 1871.   That was a
time of deeply-stirred emotion.   The much-
loved sister was going forth, a bride, from the
home of her ancestors.   It was as though a
strain of beauty and tenderness were floating
on the wind away.   Then it was, as he sat at
evensong at the royal oriel in St. George's
Chapel, gazing upon the high vault thronged
with banners, the walls inlaid with arms and
blazonry of many a famous line, that his look
was as though his spirit were kindling within

him and yearning to take rank with his fore-
fathers and heroes of a bygone day.

It was at any rate in this manner, through
the affections, through the imagination, through
personal intercourse with the representatives of
knowledge or action, that his education was in
great measure gained. The frequent troubles
of health which interfered with regular reading
never seemed to check his eagerness to see and
talk with any noteworthy man. Many visitors
to the Castle must remember interviews with
the young Prince in his rooms, interviews often
prolonged far beyond mere complimentary
limits, and leaving behind them the memory of
a listener best pleased with what was best
worth hearing, and whose transparent face
expressed that pleasure with a boy's straight-
forward charm. There might one meet Mr.
Gladstone, concentrating, perhaps, on some
morsel of Wedgwood china the great and
complex engine of his mind ; or, on a later
day, Mr. Disraeli, fresh from private audience
(December 18, 1877) and moved beyond his
wont. And from the very first it was observable how quickly the young Prince learnt from
men, how retentive was his memory for names,

for faces, for anything which had been said in
his presence ; how adroitly he fitted the pieces
into that map of the human world which all of
us carry in our heads in some fashion or other,
but which in his case came to contain so many
known points, and each in such true relation to
the rest.

His entrance at Oxford—still under the
guidance of Sir Robert Collins, his best and
lifelong friend—was a new source of interest
and excitement.   There was at first something
of pathetic wistfulness in the way in which he
regarded his joyous contemporaries, able to take
their pleasures in a fashion more active than he
could share ; but as he began to make real
intimacies his affectionate nature found full play ;
and never, perhaps, has undergraduate felt more
delightfully that first bloom of friendship which
idealises the young man's world.   Lord Brooke,
Lord Harris, Sidney Herbert, Walter Campbell,
Herbert Gladstone, and a few others, formed the
nucleus of a group which constantly widened,
and which fused together senior and junior men
with a success which, as University hosts well
know, is the highest proof of academical tact
and *bonhomie*.   He was still shy, but his shy-

ness was of that winning kind which irresistibly suggests the pleasure to be derived from overcoming it. And at Oxford he was met on all sides with a manly welcome ; the only trace (as it were by reaction) of the tuft-hunting of former days being a slight unwillingness on the part of some independent spirits to countenance one who might be suspected of wishing to approach learning by a royal road. But these men, too, were won ; nor, indeed, would they have found it easy to suggest how better to combine dignity with simplicity, or to be patrician without pride.

Among the leaders of the University Prince Leopold had many friends. The Dean of Christchurch (Dr. Liddell), Professors Rolleston, Acland, Jowett, Max Müller, Mr. Goldwin Smith, Mr. Coxe [1]—the list might be extended till most of the well-known names were told. But among all these figures there was one figure which stood alone. There was one heart to which the Prince's heart went forth with a loving reverence such as he never felt

[1] In a pre-nuptial will the Duke bequeathed his collection of autographs to the Bodleian, and the Duchess has carried out this bequest. Had he died childless, he wished his library to go to the Unattached Students of Oxford.

for any other man.   Certain colloquies of Mr.
Ruskin's at the bedside of Prince Leopold—as
he lay recovering from perilous illness, and
still in danger of a relapse—will dwell in the
mind of him who heard them as ideal examples
of the contact of an elder and a younger soul.
How close was that union in a region where
earthly rank was swept away !   How poor a
thing did any life seem then which had not
known the hallowing of sorrow !   How solemn
was that unspoken Presence which men have
miscalled Death !

From teachers, from friends, from suffering,
the Prince learnt much at Oxford.   He returned to Windsor no longer a boy but a man ;
able to take up in firmer fashion his apportioned
thread of fate.

Such, at least, was the impression given
when, a few months later, he devoted two
whole days to a methodical survey of the
Castle's treasures.   And here it was evident
how his historic interest had grown ; how in
those thousand chambers, the fabric of a score
of kings, he had learnt to decipher in brief and
summary the great story of the English race ;
from the rude helm of a Plantagenet, hanging in

some deserted gallery, to that treasure-house which holds in rich confusion the visible tokens of Queen Victoria's Indian sway—the golden gifts of Rajah and Maharajah, and tribute of the imperial East.

But the time came when it was his eager desire to have a home of his own, and to take his place in that class of country gentlemen among whom our English princes are proud to be enrolled. Boyton Manor is a typical country gentleman's home. Above it stretch the wild Wiltshire downs; beneath them the old Elizabethan manor-house stands in its terraced nook, and long glades fringed with beeches push deep into the hollowed hill. The Prince's establishment was a modest one; for his means, considering the unavoidable demands upon them, were never large, and from the time when an income of his own was accorded to him a great part of it was returned by him to the nation in subscriptions to philanthropic ends. But at Boyton he exercised much quiet hospitality, and himself gained greatly in social initiative and in the power of dealing with men and women. On the occasion of one dinner-party in particular, when several of his royal

kinsfolk were staying with him, and some of his
guests came prepared to derive honour rather
than pleasure from the entertainment, with a
simple and almost boyish grace he set the shyest
at ease, and transformed what had seemed
formidably like a royal family party into a
scene of unaffected enjoyment.   Such successes
are not wholly trifling ; they imply genuine
kindliness and alert attention ; and those who
saw the Prince beginning to regard these social
gatherings as occasions for bestowing happiness
rather than for receiving amusement, felt that
in one more direction he was learning to look
primarily to the duties rather than the pleasures
of his lot.   " Boy amongst boys, but amongst
men a man," he kept through life his youthful
freshness, though he learnt more and more to
combine with it the manlier gifts of consideration, counsel, and sympathy.

Boyton, however, was hardly more than a
transitional stage between tutelage and inde-
pendence, and it was with his removal to
Claremont in 1879 that his developed manhood
may be said to open.   It was in that year that
his individuality grew more marked and definite,
and his talk, without losing its ingenuous

boyishness, began to have substance and to show thought of his own. Here, then, it may be well to recall the upshot of many conversations, the drift of much which was habitually working in his mind during these last four active years.

The question of his public duties is best approached, as he in fact approached it, from the side of actual experience, from the consideration of what the nation does practically demand from a royal personage *en disponibilite*, from a young Prince whom it believes to be both willing and able to respond to modern needs. And it will be found that, although the new demands made on royalty may be different from the old ones, they are certainly not less onerous ; and a Prince whom circumstances preclude from war or politics is by no means driven to find his only resort in pleasure. At first sight, indeed, it might seem as though the main interests of civilised peoples gave little scope for the intervention of princes. We note the steady rise of commerce and industry, of science, art, and letters. And we observe that one group of these pursuits is unfitting for royalty, while success in the other demands

personal rather than hereditary qualifications.
But this increasing complexity of society is in
fact developing besides these a new calling of
the highest importance, and increasingly in
need of active official heads. *Philanthropy* in
the widest sense of the word, including all
organised and disinterested attempts to better
by non-political means the condition of the
nation, tends to absorb a larger and larger part
of the activity of civilised men. In fact the
proportion of national activity which is thus
directed may be taken as no bad test of the
degree of advance to which any people's civilisation has attained. This generous effort, however, tends by no means wholly to good ; much
of it is wasted on demonstrable impossibilities ;
much of it is debased by an admixture of selfish
objects ; much of it, through sheer ignorance,
does absolute harm. Philanthropy, in short, is
a field where guidance is eminently necessary,
and where experience shows that any indication
of royal approval carries immediate weight.
The multitude of applications for the use of the
Duke of Albany's name for public objects of
this kind would probably surprise every one
except those millionaires who have learnt, by

the demands made on their purses, how multifarious are modern efforts for the welfare of
mankind.

This widespread eagerness for his approval
and advocacy certainly took the Prince himself
by surprise. Thinking very modestly of his
own knowledge and powers, he was at first inclined to respond to few of such appeals, and only
where he felt that some special taste or interest
of his own gave him a right to a decided opinion.
But he gradually recognised that this was not
really all which his post in the world demanded
of him. He began to enter into the ideal
which his wise father had perhaps been the
first among royal personages distinctly to conceive and steadily to apply—the ideal of royalty
as a source of disinterested counsel and encouragement, not thrust upon a nation, but
always ready when desired, and representing
thus some part of the old *paternal* function which,
as nations grow to manhood, must needs
change its character or disappear. The
peculiarity of the Prince Consort's position
prevented his great qualities from being rapidly
realised ; and the nation lost him before it
knew him well enough to feel all the gratitude

which he deserved. Prince Leopold, on the
other hand, had the inestimable advantage of
being his mother's son as well as his father's,
and of beginning life with an unlimited draft
of credit on England's affection and respect.
And he became gradually aware that the nation
was demanding of *him*, almost beyond his
powers, that which he felt that his father would
have been able to supply so much more fully
than was in his time demanded, namely, a kind
of headship of philanthropy, a guidance and
encouragement of the manifold efforts which
our age is making towards a higher and purer
life. A selfish or a timid man might shrink
from such a responsibility as this ; a foolish or
a vain man might degrade it by supporting
mere favourites and advocating mere crotchets
of his own. But from vanity of this kind
Prince Leopold was completely free. He had
by no means an exaggerated opinion of his
own powers ; and when he heard his abilities
or character ranked with his father's, he was
merely pained to think how much of the credit
due to the originator of a wise line of thought
or conduct is often diverted to a successor
whom circumstances enable to carry out the

pregnant suggestion in a popular and conspicuous way. Fortunately this very modesty,
simplicity, straightforwardness of character
were precisely what was most needed in the
Prince's position. For what the public expects
a royal opinion to represent is not simply an
individual preference, however refined or ingeni-
ous, but rather a kind of *résumé* or outcome
of the best opinions held at the time. Just as
a great newspaper gains its power by subor-
dinating to "the common sense of most" all
personal predilection or whim, so a princely
supporter of schemes of public welfare will
carry permanent weight only if the public feels
that it can count on his position as a real
guarantee of impersonality, of detachment not
only from unworthy motives, but from every
kind of prepossession or crotchet. His business
is not to be a special pleader, but an arbitrator ;
not an explorer, but a map-maker ; not to lead
revolutions in opinion, but to confer a *de jure*
title on opinions which are rapidly acquiring a
de facto sway.

This was not altogether an attractive pro-
gramme for a young man of spirit. To say
nothing from the impulse of the moment to

write nothing without the gravest deliberation, to enforce accepted truths and sanction winning causes—there may seem little in such work which can be embraced with enthusiasm. Yet here again the voluntary acceptance of limitations is soon seen to render possible the achievement of most important good. Though only those causes be supported which a consensus of careful opinion pronounces to be both deserving of success and likely to attain it, the field of choice is still very large. And sometimes (as was the case, for instance, with the question of parks, open spaces, preservation of the Lake-country from railways, etc., in which Mr. Ruskin's influence was discernible), the ultimate success of some philanthropic effort can be safely predicted at a very early stage by those who make it a business to watch all such efforts as they arise, to study their inter-relation, and to know something of the character of their supporters. Assuredly there is work here— work earnestly demanded and gratefully welcomed by the nation—for as many public-spirited princes as any reigning family can supply.

Moreover, there is another branch of this

work more onerous than any task for tongue or pen. If a great personage wishes to give the full weight of his support to any cause, it is often necessary that he should be actually stamped on the popular retina in visible connection with it, actually looked at hour after hour while the cause is kept before the minds of men. It is obvious that for this function royalty is uniquely fitted, and Prince Leopold recognised to the full that this must form a large element in his life. Some eminent examples have accustomed the public to so high a standard of royal vigour that the fatigue of these duties of ceremony and *representation* is scarcely realised by ordinary observers. To Prince Leopold's delicate constitution those fatigues were most severe, though he met them with readiness, and would only jestingly allude to the inconvenience of holding one's hat three inches above one's head for a couple of hours in an east wind, or to the pains which he took to catch some one's eye in the crowd each time that he bowed and smiled, till his head grew too dizzy and his cheeks too strained for more than an automatic salute.

The Duke of Albany desired, as is known, a

sphere of activity of a more definite kind. It was a bitter disappointment to him that he was not permitted to succeed Lord Lorne in Canada, and it was long before he could heartily acquiesce in the interdiction from this high duty which reasons of State imposed. But here again he did at last acquiesce, and recognised also ·that the task would have involved too severe a strain on his physical powers. He still hoped some day to fill what seemed a less fatiguing position of the same kind in Australia ; and the aspiration indicated his desire for serious and regular work, as well as his deep interest in that great process of expansion which is carrying our England into every quarter of the globe.

On the whole, then, it may be said that in public matters his brief career was a progressive self-adjustment to the conditions of his lot, a growing acceptance of duty, and not caprice or pleasure, as the guide of life. So far as he achieved this, he attained happiness ; and so far as sickness and suffering helped him to achieve it, they were the blessings of his life.

For aid in this conversion of pain into education, of restraint into guidance, the late

Prince devoutly sought the grace and influence of a higher Power. A loyal son of the Church, he retained through life much of the simple piety of his boyish years. But to say this is not enough. The Prince had learnt at the gates of death a sense of the reality of the Unseen which many theologians might envy. "The untravelled traveller" had brought back with him from that bourne, so nearly overpassed, a conviction, into whose intimate basis it would have been over-curious to pry, of the near, the interpenetrating presence of a spiritual world. And like most men for whom these great conceptions have passed from an "article of faith" to what may almost be called a fact of experience, he could scarcely understand the difficulty felt by other minds in attaining to a certainty like his own. He longed that they should see things as he saw them ; that they should feel the validity of every class of evidence which points to this world's confusion as transitory, and to death as a liberation and not a close.

This practical manner of viewing speculative topics showed itself in an interesting way when, some two years before his death, a society was

founded which had for its object to investigate,
on strictly scientific principles, and without prepossession of any kind, those obscure and
scattered facts or fancies which point to the
existence of an unseen or immaterial principle
in man.   Although it would obviously have been
unfitting for the Prince to have lent his name to
a study so novel and tentative, his sympathies
with the effort thus initiated were very warm.
Yet even in this speculative region his point of
view was philanthropic rather than scientific.
Himself intimately convinced of the existence
of a soul in man, he readily assumed that a
candid and organised inquiry would sooner or
later convince other minds also.   What he
desired, then, was that any scientific evidence
which could be gained as to the soul and a
future life should be actively brought to bear on
the masses who in many parts of the world are
losing those beliefs altogether.   Russian Nihil-
ism and German Socialism loom large before
the eyes of princes ; and it is obvious enough
how direct in these cases is the relation between
disbelief in a future life and reckless rebellion
against the laws and limitations which hedge
round the only existence for which these poor

men hope.   Prince Leopold can certainly not
be accused of wishing to still the cry of the poor
and miserable in this life by presenting them
with a blank cheque on an unknown futurity.
But, while eager to ameliorate and cheer the
lives of the poor in every possible way, he was
conscious that " the hope of a better resurrection "
was in their case especially needful, both as a
background of contentment and as a stimulus
to well-doing.   And perceiving, as a mere
matter of fact, that great masses of men, in
Germany especially, are becoming less and less
disposed to accept the validity of religious
instinct and historical tradition—more and more
resolved to trust such teaching only as can base
itself on contemporary experience and appeal to
tangible experiment—he earnestly desired that
the dignitaries of great churches, the leaders of
all sections of religious thought, should welcome
any prospect of an alliance with scientific discovery, and convert to the upbuilding of the
higher life those modern modes of thought
which have sometimes been pursued to its prejudice, or been held to have proved its
unreality.

But there is some danger lest such a discus-

sion as this should give the impression of a more
sustained seriousness than his conversation
actually showed. The trains of thought above
indicated did indeed exist in his mind, but they
came out in no set fashion, and only in intimate moments ; while no man more thoroughly
enjoyed the lighter talk of society, and its lively
comment on the personages and events of the
day. One thing was specially noticeable in his
pleasant, humorous chat, and that was his
tendency to think as well as possible of almost
every woman of his acquaintance. He who
thus cares for the womanhood in women is
rewarded by wider and keener interests than are
felt by the man whose admirations have a
selfish taint. From the society of the old, and
of young children, the Duke derived especial
pleasure. Few brothers have held their sisters
so dear ; nor did he ever talk intimately on
these matters without introducing some affectionate allusion to his nieces at Darmstadt.

This quick susceptibility to feminine charm
and virtue, while it makes a man more likely to
choose well in marriage, makes it also eminently
desirable that he should have the best possible
range of choice. Here, too, there were limita-

tions in the Prince's lot ; here, too, there was a
period of discontent and disheartenment; and
here, too, the old lesson was repeated on a larger
scale ; the restriction of choice became its guidance, and the most perfect of love-matches
blossomed on royal soil. How eagerly did
those who knew the all-importance to the Duke
of domestic happiness watch for the first glimpse
of the bride in St. George's Chapel ! with what
thankfulness did they read in that face the
heaven-made marriage, and the soul to his
akin !

Πάραντα δ' ἐλθεῖν ἐς Ἰλίου πόλιν·
λέγοιμ' ἂν φρόνημα μὲν νηνέμου γαλάνας.

With her came tranquillity and contentment,
the deep satisfaction of the heart ;—what *seemed*
a hold upon the earthly future, what *was* but a
flying foretaste of the stability of a serener
world. The life of Claremont, till then expectant and provisional, rounded itself into
happy wholeness, and its master threw himself with new energy into all that could adorn
the home which the Queen's gift and his wife's
companionship had made his own indeed, so
far as transitory man can find his haven in these
possessions of a day. The birth of his child

was a completing joy, and he loved to picture
Claremont to himself as destined to become one
of those great English homes which knit together sexes, ages, ranks of life, nay, even
animals and men, in a closer and more patri
archal polity than the modern world elsewhere
knows ; where the same tranquillity of well-
being pervades mansion, stables, farm ; while
the master's central presence is felt as the
strength and stay of all, and radiates an ordering
beneficence from fence to fence of the domain.

Claremont is a noble setting for such a life.
The house itself is large and stately, but it is
the park and woodland which make the special
character of the place.   For through the sorrows
and the vicissitudes which have passed over the
majestic home—the self-sought death of the
founder of an empire, the sad retirement of
exiled monarchs, the extinction in mother and
infant at once of a great nation's proudest hope
—through all these seasons Nature has worked
unseen ; the woods have spread, the shadows
deepened ; great pines have reared themselves
in sombre pyramids, and flowering shrubs have
met and tangled in an undergrowth of bloom
and green.

Hoc nemus, hunc, inquit, frondoso vertice collem—
Quis deus incertum est—habitat deus.

The domain of Claremont, its solitary solemnity,
the gloom of its embosomed glades, recalls some
seat of oracle where ancient men adored an un-
apparent divinity, uncertain between love and
fear, nor knew whose whisper rolled in the
woodlands, whose form had been guessed amid
the shade.

But with the coming of that home's mistress
all omens gave their sign for peace. The two
together, one in heart, in aspiration, in duty,
desired that the happy life which the nation's
gift supported should be such in every detail
that the whole nation might look on it if it
would, and recognise royalty only by its
graciousness, and elevation by its repose. It
was their hope gradually to make Claremont
a rallying-point, not of rank or fashion merely,
but of whatever was best and highest in every
direction, invoking the arts and graces of life,—
music especially, for which the Prince himself
had so true a gift,—to make a society that
should be delightful without false excitement, a
stately but simple home. Lives thus wisely led
by other highly-placed personages the Duke

watched always with sympathetic interest. And
in certain graver matters of social governance
in which the last appeal lies sometimes to
royalty alone, he would dwell with admiration
on the judgment and firmness which his eldest
brother had shown in many cases where the
heads of an aristocratic society may, by their
potent intervention at critical moments, largely
determine the welfare of other lives.

How much of influence might in time have
come to that home's master we cannot know ;
but we may be sure that whatever had come to
him would in this temper have been exerted
well. For just as learning and wealth and
beauty are odious or beneficent, according as
their possessors have realised aright that their
learning was not given them for pride, nor
their wealth for luxury, nor their beauty for
adulation ; so also may royal rank become an
unmixed source of happiness when they who
hold it have learnt to account themselves not
as the depositaries of privilege, but as the
channels of honour. For it is not the orator
only who " receives from the multitude in a
vapour what he returns to them in a flood,"
but the great House with which our English

nation has identified her name and fortunes
receives the convergent rays of a world-wide
and immemorial affection, which it is the royal
task to focus in a steady glow, directing back
on what is best and worthiest in all our empire the warmth and light which were derived
diffusedly from every heart within that empire's
bound.   The Duke of Albany felt this to the
utmost,—and he felt, too, with almost painful
vividness the generous abundance of the recognition which England gave to his efforts for
her good.   It was his nature to think that any
other man in his position would have worked
harder and done better than he ; and he was
often depressed at the thought of his insuffici-
ency to repay the confidence of such a multitude
of men.

For, indeed, he hardly recognised the
strength of the attachment which his own
character and presence inspired.   He was
always afraid that his friends would grow tired
of him ; that they would become absorbed in
other interests ; that they would marry and
come and see him no more.   At the height of
his popularity his manner kept a certain wistfulness, as if he were asking for an affection

on which he had no right to rely. He did not
know how dear to others was his soft laugh of
sympathy, his steady gaze of affection, the
sound of his gentle speech,—the ἀγανοφροσύνη
—the loving-kindness—which his friends may
now seek far and mournfully, and whose remem-
brance fills their eyes with tears.

And then, too, how high was their hope!
What years of usefulness and honour seemed
opening before him they loved!   Still was
Mr. Ruskin the honoured teacher ; still was
it possible to watch, in fuller maturity, the
contact of the elder and the younger
mind.   Who could help thinking of Plato's
great conception, where the spirit which once
has looked on truth in the wake of some
divinity in the ideal world seeks out on earth
the awakening intelligence most apt to follow,
and fashions that young life to greatness, " after
the likeness of his tutelary god " ?   It seemed
as though that teacher—who, if any man, has
" gazed in clear radiance on visions innocent
and fair,"—had found a " royal soul " to whom
to prophesy, and from whose answering fervour
virtue and blessing might be born.

But it was not best that this should be

Not in this world of shows, but in the world of realities, was the next lesson to be taught to that advancing soul. The earthly bliss dissolved in a moment, the earthly promise vanished like a dream. Only in the vistas of that beechen woodland, and in that vale of rhododendrons, and by that still water's edge where the gigantic forest-trees " high overarched imbower," pictures from the past will live imprinted on one woman's heart ; pictures enduring beneath their apparent transiency, and indissoluble by any touch of change. It is not the ebb and flow of common hours which traces the limit of our being, but the flood-tide on which the soul has once swept forward leaves the wave-mark which she can reach for evermore.

Those who believe, not in word only, but in deed and in truth, in the great destiny of enfranchised souls, will not need to *compassionate* any true and upright spirit which is called away, however suddenly, from a life however sweet. He may leave wife, and child, and fame, and fortune, but duty and virtue are with him still, and that peremptory call is an upward summons, a step in his high career.

R

With the survivors of the well-beloved son, brother, husband, the whole world will mourn. Yet such a death is a stingless sorrow. No parting can sever the spiritual bond which the strong heart chooses to maintain ; what love has lost in joy it has gained in consecration ; it is uplifted at one stroke among flawless and eternal things. Thus shall even his nearest and dearest feel as the years roll by ; thus too let others feel who from a distance share and reverence their sorrow ; others—for whom also the falling of that handful of light earth into the flower-strewn vault marked the earthly close of an irreplaceable, a unique affection —the conversion of one of life's best delights into a memory and an anticipation—nay, the transference of a part of the very heart itself from the visible into that ideal world where such as he are more than princes, and where all high hopes find their goal.

In the Wolsey Chapel, Windsor.

Prince well-beloved ! true heart and presence fair !
    High o'er the marble of thy carved repose
    From Windsor's Keep the Flag of England
        blows ;
A thousand years float in the storied air.
There sleeps thy Sire ; and often gently there
    Comes one who mourns with steadfast eyes, and
        strows
    The rhododendron round thee and the rose ,
Love is her silence and her look is prayer.
Nor now that Banner's broad-flung triumphings,
Nor spirit whispering to the sons of kings
    Of strong continuance, age-long empery ;—
But that one woman's gaze the promise brings
To thee that sleepest of eternal things,
    Realms yet unreached, and high love still to be.

THE END

Printed by R. & R. Clark, *Edinburgh.*

For EU product safety concerns, contact us at Calle de José Abascal, 56–1°,
28003 Madrid, Spain or eugpsr@cambridge.org.